MW01600852

Try to Block Me; You Can't Stop Me!
Roy Daniels Murray Jr.
Published by TW & CO Publishing

Copyright 2025 CI-40547460529
ISBN: 9798296392855

Printed in the U.S.A.

DEDICATION

Dedicated to all the descendants of Phyllis Cruel, your strength, faith, and perseverance live on through us. May we honor your legacy with courage, unity, and purpose for generations to come.

CONTENTS

Try to Block Him; You Can't Stop Him!

My Dad *by Roy Daniels Murray Jr.*

Try to block him; you can't stop him.

Not just a father to me, but a father to the community he

would be.

Born in the county, where education was limited.

He walked to school to Liberty on a Hill.

And moved from Miss to Miss, and high school he

fulfilled.

He didn't stop there; in the Army he landed.

Then off to college; several degrees he commanded.

A high school graduate, a Master's plus 30,

When others gave up, he got down and dirty.

Try to block him; you can't stop him.

Not just a motivator to me, but a motivator to the

community he would be.

He married his sweetheart, and four children later,

He didn't stop there, he would not dare.

He taught school, cut hair, and shined shoes.

A Masonic lodge he joined, the NAACP he adorned.

A garden he plowed, a family he raised, a team he coached.

A community activist, a husband, a father.

From his garden, a community he fed.

From his heart, a community he led.

Try to block him; you can't stop him.

Not just an educator to me, but an educator to the

community he would be.

On his life, a calling came.

He returned back to Liberty without a blame.

A speaker, a preacher, a pastor,

A mentor, a guide, a master.

Try to block him; you can't stop him.

Not just a leader to me, but a leader to the community he

would be.

Now I must skip ahead, or all day we would be here

instead.

A pandemic hit, a world was submerged.

A circle was formed,

A teacher, a preacher, a motivator emerged.

A wasp did fly, a hip did break, but . . .

Try to block him; you can't stop him.

Not just a pillar of strength to me, but a pillar of strength to

the community he would be.

FOREWORD

BY ROY DANIELS MURRAY JR.

This book was born out of love, for my father, for our family, and for the story he carried inside him for nearly a century.

I grew up hearing the stories. They were never just tales, they were lessons wrapped in rhythm, humor, and memory. My father, Roy Daniels Murray Sr., didn't just live through history, he carried it, preached it, taught it, and passed it down to us like sacred scripture. He told us about the cotton fields and the kerosene lamps, about chopping wood and walking barefoot to school, about the cruelty of segregation and the strength of community. He told us about Phyllis Cruel, our great-great-grandmother, who was born a slave, and about Papa Alfred, who built a life from red dirt and resilience. He made us understand that we didn't come from nothing, we came from everything.

This project started with recordings. Long conversations. Sometimes structured, sometimes just rambling stories over coffee or a phone call. At first, I just wanted to capture his voice before time stole it from us. But the more we recorded, the more I realized: this wasn't just *his* story. It was *our* story. It was the story of how a Black boy born in 1929 in the Jim Crow South became a man of faith, a builder of family, a teacher of generations, and a living testimony to God's grace.

I had to get his story told. Not because he asked me to, in fact, he never did, but because I knew if I didn't do it, the world might never understand what kind of miracle this man was. The world might never see how a man who picked cotton as a boy went on to educate thousands, raise a family of strong-willed, faith-filled children, and pastor churches into his '90s. The world might never know how many people he counseled in his barber chair, how many young men he pulled from the edge with just a word, a joke, a prayer. The world might never know how deeply he loved, and how deeply he was loved.

This book is more than a memoir. It's a map. A survival guide. A testimony. And it's my offering back to the man who gave me everything: my name, my values, my sense of purpose.

Daddy always taught us to know where we came from. He said, "*If you don't know your past, you'll trip over your future.*" So this is the past, preserved, protected, and passed down. May it guide every step ahead.

To the readers, thank you for walking with us. You're not just reading history, you're holding a life that mattered. And to my father: this is for you. I don't believe He brought you this far to leave you, and I don't believe He brought me this far without calling me to tell your story.

Roy Daniels Murray Jr.
Shreveport, Louisiana
2025

THE ENTRANCE

As far back as I can remember, my ancestry begins with my great-grandmother, Phyllis Cruel. Born into slavery in 1832 in Virginia, Phyllis bore the last name of her master, a name that mocked her freedom even as it claimed ownership over her body. She labored endlessly under the Southern sun, not just picking cotton and working the fields but enduring the unspeakable pain of bearing five children, Minnie, George, Sarah, Martha, and Tobe, fathered by her enslaver. This horror was not rare. It was the cruel rhythm of slavery, where White men crowned their wives as society's finest while treating Black women as property to be used in the dark. The plantation was both a workplace and prison, and its cruelty reached every corner of life. Enslaved people were stripped of their names, their dignity, and their dreams, brought to America not for citizenship but for servitude, solely to build the wealth of their oppressors. Reflecting on these brutal truths still burns in my chest, even today. But despite that pain, I hold onto something else: the unshakable determination of our ancestors. They survived the lash and the chains and still managed to protect a seed of hope that would grow through generations.

When slavery was abolished, Phyllis did not look back. She left that Virginia plantation with her five children in tow, and the only thing the master left her was his name. But she didn't carry that name in shame. She carried it as a witness. A reminder of what had been taken and what would never be taken again. Somewhere along her journey, she met and married Jacob Daniels, a strong and resolute Black man from Virginia. I do not know how a woman and a man from Virginia found themselves in Caddo Parish, Louisiana. That part of the story remains shrouded in silence, like so many Black family histories interrupted by slavery. But on January 9, 1870, they married, free at last and forging a new path. Their union didn't just create a family, it planted roots in Louisiana soil that would grow into fields of legacy. Their story, though clouded by injustice, is ultimately one of hope, of faith, and of a future imagined beyond the plantation gates.

Jacob, known to many as Jake Daniels, and Phyllis Cruel Daniels had one son: Alfred Daniels, my maternal grandfather. He was born on February 13, 1869, just a few years after President Abraham Lincoln signed the Emancipation Proclamation. Though the ink on that historic document had begun to dry, its promise was still fresh, and fragile, in the hearts of newly freed Black families. Alfred entered this world as a free man, but just barely. He was born in the long shadow of slavery and the uncertain dawn of Reconstruction. Still, his very existence was a declaration of survival and possibility. In a time when freedom for Black people was still being contested at every turn, Alfred Daniels stood as a quiet beacon, a firstborn of hope, anchored in the soil of the South.

Alfred would later marry Clifford Bradley, a woman of deep character whose family roots are mostly hidden in the fog of history. What I do know is that her parents were William and Louisiana Bradley, and from them, she inherited a quiet strength that would carry her through the demands of marriage, motherhood, and life in the post-slavery South. Alfred and Clifford were joined in marriage on December 5, 1892, and together, they built their home in Bienville Parish, a place that would later come to be known more intimately as Loggy Bayou. Their house, like many of that era, was more than a shelter, it was the heart of their family. It pulsed with life, with the daily stir of eleven children who reached adulthood and the aching silence left by two little ones lost in early childhood. Back then, large families were both a blessing and a necessity. Each child was another set of hands in the fields, another voice at the table, another light in the darkness. The system of sharecropping had taken the place of slavery, but it still bound Black families to the land in hardship. Yet Alfred and Clifford made a way. Their home was a place of work, yes, but also of warmth, worship, and the enduring rhythm of love passed down.

My mother, Lucille Daniels, was born on October 25, 1893, the firstborn child of Alfred and Clifford Daniels. As the eldest, she bore the weight of responsibility early and often, setting the rhythm for her ten younger siblings who followed in quick succession: Mary, Alfred Jr., Ophelia, Rufus, Doris, Ralph, Luther Helen, Clifford, and J. C. In those days, the eldest daughter wasn't just a child, she was a second mother, a caregiver in a house full of mouths to feed, clothes to mend, and lessons to teach by example. Lucille grew into her role with quiet strength, shaped by the order of farm life and the unspoken expectation that she would always do what was proper and necessary.

Sometime around 1925, she married my father, Bates Murray. The story of how they met has been lost to time, swallowed by the years and the silences our elders often kept. But I remember him vividly. My father had served in the United States Army during World War I, and he carried the presence of a man who had seen things he didn't talk about. His past hung around him like smoke, visible, heavy, but never fully explained. In our house, there were objects that seemed to hold pieces of his story: a gas mask, stiff and alien, and a military uniform, pressed and folded like it still held command. Both sat tucked away in the closet, but to me, they might as well have been ghosts. I would stare at them, heart pounding, imagining the war he had been through and the things he refused to say.

My parents stayed together for eight years after my birth on July 18, 1929. Their eventual separation was not loud or violent, it was quiet, like a slow unraveling you only notice after the thread has already come loose. To this day, the reasons remain unspoken, buried beneath layers of pride, pain, and silence. But what I do remember, what I can never forget, is that my father, Bates Murray, was a man shaped, and likely shattered, by the war. He had served in World War I, and while he came back wearing a uniform, something in him never truly returned. His presence in our home was like fog, there but distant. His silence wasn't empty; it was thick, weighted with things he would never say. That gas mask and military uniform, hanging still and cold in the closet, became symbols of his absence. Just the sight of that mask sent chills through my body. At night, I'd lie in bed, eyes wide open, haunted by the very things meant to protect him. Eventually, I'd crawl into the crowded bed I shared with my three brothers. There, pressed together in that narrow space, we found warmth, not just against the cold, but against the fear. My father's trauma didn't just live in his mind. It seeped into our home, touching everything and everyone.

He was not a provider in the traditional sense. But the true loss wasn't measured in food or money, it was measured in presence. He was there, but not really. And that absence, both physical and spiritual, left a hollow space inside me that no amount of time or success has ever fully closed. Still, I learned to carry that emptiness without letting it define me; I bore it the way my ancestors bore their burdens, with a quiet strength forged through suffering and passed down like a family heirloom. They carried chains and cotton sacks. I carried silence and longing. The weight was different, but the resilience was the same.

My mother, Lucille, stood in that gap. She was the one who kept us going when the center fell apart. Together, she and my father had five children: Bates Jr., Lee Arthur, Clifford, Katherine, and me, Roy. Even before the separation, Mama worked herself to the bone. She cooked and cleaned for wealthy White families who barely acknowledged her presence, let alone her dignity. After long days spent making other people's lives easier, she came home to tend to us, five Black children trying to understand a father who was there but unreachable, and to face the sharp edges of a man no war had ever softened. Whether the harm he caused was physical or emotional, it hung over our house like smoke, silent, choking, always lingering.

We lived in Shreveport, Louisiana, and like many Black families in the city, we moved often, always searching for better, safer, cheaper. The addresses blurred together, but Taylor Court Street remains sharp in my memory. Our house stood just behind the Doctor's Hospital. I can still see those bodies falling from the hospital windows, men and women who had either jumped or been pushed. As a boy, I'd press my head to the glass and wait, stomach tight, for someone to roll down into our backyard. I didn't understand mental illness or despair, but I understood fear. And I lived with it, inside and outside the house.

But the real threat didn't just fall from the sky, it came with a blueprint. Our neighborhood was later targeted by the state's plan to expand Interstate I-20. It was a familiar story playing out in cities all over America, Black neighborhoods declared expendable in the name of "progress." Bulldozers came through like judgment, flattening homes, splitting up families, burying memories beneath fresh concrete. They said it was infrastructure. We knew better. It was erasure, plain and deliberate. The streets we grew up on disappeared. Our front porches turned to on-ramps. And just like that, a piece of our history was stolen and paved over without apology.

But long before concrete buried our block, something quieter had begun to collapse inside our home. The breaking didn't come with bulldozers, it came with long silences, averted eyes, and the weight of things that were never said. Our neighborhood was being torn down by policy, but our family was unraveling under pressure that couldn't be traced on any map. The two losses, public and private, felt different but cut just as deep.

We didn't just leave a man, we left a memory, a rhythm, a routine that had worn itself threadbare. The kind of change Mama made wasn't just logistical, it was spiritual. We didn't pack much, but we carried everything: sorrow, resilience, and a kind of quiet courage born from generations before us. At the same time, the rest of the world was grappling with its own kind of fracture. While the nation tried to claw its way out of the Great Depression, rural Black families like ours knew better than to wait on Washington. In the South, survival didn't come from a government program, it came from gardens, pine knots, and the calloused hands of men who worked the land they'd never own. We didn't have bank loans or cotton subsidies; we had each other.

And while we leaned on each other, we did so under the looming shadow of Jim Crow. In places like Bienville Parish, the laws weren't just unjust, they were enforced viciously and reminded us daily that we were not free. The police, the courts, even the local sheriffs, all were instruments of white supremacy. Justice for Black folks was rare. Protection under the law? Nonexistent. In 1937 alone, lynchings across the South were frequent and unpunished. It didn't take much, an accusation, a glance, a refusal to yield, to spark a mob and end a life. We lived with that fear. It hummed underneath every conversation, every decision.

And for Mama, that fear wasn't theoretical; it was lived, daily and up close. It wasn't just the danger outside that pressed on her spirit, but the unrest inside our home. She knew the world could take everything if she didn't act. So she did.

So in 1937, Mama returned to the only place where we had a fighting chance: her father's house. Papa's house wasn't paradise, but it was protection. It was where my mother could raise her children without the crack of a soldier's rage echoing through the house, a place where we lived off the land, lit kerosene lamps, and warmed ourselves by fire, because Black families in the South have always known how to make something from nothing.

Her decision to leave wasn't just about leaving a man, it was about rejecting a world of violence and claiming one of dignity. Just as Black communities protected themselves from the terror outside their homes, my mother protected us from the terror inside ours. In doing so, she aligned herself with a larger movement of Black women across the South who resisted oppression not with protest signs but with pots of beans on wood stoves, with stitched quilts, and with the simple act of choosing safety over silence.

BACK TO GRANDFATHER'S HOUSE

My Papa's house was on a patch of land just outside of Ringgold, also called Loggy Bayou, in the deep woods of Bienville Parish, no paved streets, no light poles, no town clock. Ringgold was the closest town to where we'd go for supplies. But our life played out on the land, quiet, rugged, and full of lessons you couldn't learn in the city. His house was not the most lavish, but it was peaceful and wrapped around you like a well-worn quilt. It didn't need chandeliers or polished floors, what it had was soul. It was the kind of place where you could take a deep breath and let your shoulders drop because you knew you were safe. "Papa" is what we called our grandfather, and that name didn't just belong to us, it belonged to the whole family. He was Papa to his children, to his grandchildren, and to anyone who needed a father figure or a place to land. Papa's house was home, and he opened it freely to whoever needed shelter, rest, or simply to feel like they belonged.

The house had a long central hallway that ran from the front porch to the back door, like a spine holding the body of the home together. On either side of that hall were rooms that told the story of our family, each one filled with memories, smells, and people. To the left were two rooms. The first belonged to my grandfather and grandmother, Papa Alfred and Mama Clifford. Their room was quiet, warm, and heavy with the feeling of years lived and struggles survived. Next to their room was one that belonged to Uncle JC, the youngest of the family. That space held its own rhythm until he finally moved out, at which point my brothers, and I took it over, turning it into a boy's domain filled with whispers, wrestling, and shared secrets. Across the hall, my mother and sisters lived in the first room on the right. That room had a fireplace. Later, a wooden heater was installed to replace a faulty fireplace that had once been known to catch fire without warning. That fireplace didn't just keep the room warm, it made it the emotional heart of the house during the cold seasons.

The kitchen was next to my mother's and sister's room, the soul of any Southern home. It had a wood-burning stove that filled the space with the smell of cornbread, fried salt pork, or beans simmering in an iron pot. That room was not large by today's standards, but to us, it was more than enough. It was where my mother stood after a long day, where siblings crowded around to taste something off a wooden spoon, and where the family gathered when we needed to be fed, physically and emotionally. The kitchen, like every room in Papa's house, was functional, worn, and full of love. In that house, with its creaking floors and open doors, I learned what it truly meant to be held by family.

After living in the country at my grandfather's house for a few months, it was finally time for me to learn something that every country boy had to know, how to start a fire using pine knots. It wasn't just a chore, it was a rite of passage.

Papa called for me one cold morning and handed me the task like it was sacred. I observed as the older boys showed me how to slice the pine knots into smaller, dry, resin-rich pieces. After cutting them down, you'd douse just a little kerosene on the pile, strike a match, and stand back as the flames curled up and caught hold. It amazed me. The process was almost like magic. Growing up in the city, I had never lit a fire before. We turned knobs on stoves and flipped light switches on the wall. But out here in the country, nothing came easy. Everything had to be earned, lit, chopped, fetched, or grown. Still, something about that first fire stirred something in me. I felt like I was learning how to survive.

We didn't have electricity, so kerosene lamps became our primary light source at night. But even kerosene was hard to come by. It was treated like treasure, used sparingly, measured carefully. On cold winter nights when the lamp oil ran low, we used the chimney before it was replaced for warmth and light. The glow of the fire, soft and golden, would dance across the wooden walls, throwing long shadows into the corners. Most houses in the countryside had one chimney, but some of the bigger ones had two, one in the kitchen, the other in the front hall, or another room. Ours had just one, and it worked double duty.

In the kitchen, the wood stove was slightly smaller than the fireplace, so the wood we used there had to be split thinner and stacked neatly. But the chimney was where we built our long-lasting fires. I remember placing a massive piece of wood at the very back, what we called the backlog, and then building a small, steady fire in the front. That backlog would burn slow and low, feeding the fire like a heartbeat all night long. It was efficient, silent, and powerful, just like the people who taught me how to do it.

At the time, I didn't realize that our way of life was shaped by forces far beyond our little plot of land. The Great Depression may have officially ended, but its grip still lingered, especially for Black families in the South. Crop prices were low, cotton, in particular, had crashed, and the sharecropping system had evolved into a new kind of economic bondage. Most folks were farming land they didn't own, working from sunup to sundown on someone else's promise, hoping it might one day lead to something of their own. But not us. My Papa owned the land we worked. That made us different. That made us blessed. The federal government introduced New Deal relief programs, but they rarely made their way to us. Local White officials controlled who got aid and who didn't, and most of the time, we didn't. Instead of waiting for help that never came, we did what we always had: we relied on each other.

Oddly enough, some of the most challenging tasks became moments of joy. Collecting wood, chopping it, and hunting for pine knots turned into something more than a chore. For a young boy with a big imagination, it was like a treasure hunt. I'd laugh and wrestle with my older brothers in the woods, turning work into play. As I got older, my responsibilities grew, hauling, stacking, tending the fire. But I didn't mind. Being busy made me feel like I mattered. It meant I was contributing, not just watching. In those small acts, sweating, building, preparing, I was beginning to learn what it meant to be a man.

I remember studying my school lessons by the chimney, my notebook resting on my lap, the flicker of firelight dancing across the page. The warm, roaring glow from the hearth gave us both heat and illumination, especially during the long winter nights when the wind whispered through the cracks in the walls and the chill settled into our bones. The houses in the countryside were dark and cold in the winter, and without electricity, we had to make do with what we had. But somehow, those moments didn't feel like suffering. In fact, they became some of my earliest memories of peace. It might sound strange, but sitting there, reading aloud with my brothers and sisters, felt like the first authentic taste of joy I'd known since leaving Shreveport and my father's shadow behind. Even studying felt like entertainment, not because it was easy, but because it was shared. Because it was safe. And more than anything, it was ours. With each passing day in Papa's house, Mama seemed lighter, more like herself again. And as her spirit lifted, so did ours. A mother's peace has a way of settling into an entire household.

While we were returning to Ringgold, thousands of other Black families across the South packed up and headed in the opposite direction. The Great Migration was already in motion, men, women, and children loading up wagons, trains, and later buses, chasing the hope of jobs, justice, and dignity in northern and western cities. The South, still tangled in Jim Crow laws, lynchings, and economic oppression, was bleeding out its Black population. Mechanized cotton pickers had begun creeping into the fields, signaling the death knell for sharecropping and tenant farming as we knew it. The few jobs that had barely sustained Black families were disappearing, replaced by machines, and managed by White landowners who saw no future for us. Trapped in cycles of debt peonage, many saw no choice but to leave. But not us. While others headed north for opportunity, we turned back, to Papa's house, to the dirt and the pine trees, to family. We weren't running from the South but returning to reclaim it. For us, the answer wasn't flight, it was rootedness. We came back not just for a roof over our heads but for something more profound: stability, identity, and the sacred sense of belonging that only comes from standing where your people have stood for generations. The people in our community were resilient. They had to be. Winters were brutal, and most families spent them with barely any heat. We bundled up, crowded around the fire, and carried on. Summers, on the other hand, were sweltering. The days stretched long and hot, and we spent most of them outside, barefoot, shirtless, and sweating, whether working in the fields or just chasing each other down red dirt roads. Shoes were a luxury we often went without. At night, the house would open itself to the outside. Every window stood wide, inviting in the slightest hint of a breeze. We'd lie on top of the covers, sticky with the heat but tired in a way that only fresh air and hard work could bring. That's just how it was, simple, complex, and holy in its own way.

Papa possessed a well, and to us, it may as well have been a miracle in the yard. That well was our only source of fresh water, and though I never knew who dug it or when it was dug, it had been there for as long as I could remember. It stood like a sentinel in the yard, deep, quiet, and magical, offering life to the whole household. We didn't have pipes or faucets; we had that well. A rope, coarse and darkened by years of use, was wrapped around a wooden cylinder suspended over the shaft. It spun smoothly and effortlessly, like it had been greased by the hands of time. Lowering the bucket took strength and care, and as it descended into the darkness below, we would listen for the splash that told us we had reached the water's surface. Then came the pulling, drawing the water back up, hand over hand, the rope burning against our palms in summer and stiff with frost in winter. We called it exactly what it was: drawing a bucket of water. And though it was a daily task, it never lost its quiet reverence. That water didn't just quench thirst, it nourished us, body and soul.

At the end of the hall inside Papa's house sat another water bucket resting on a small wooden shelf. This bucket was filled each day by one of us boys. Papa didn't ask twice, he just called out, firm and clear, "Go draw a bucket of water!" Whoever he called that day knew the job was theirs. The well water came up cold and crisp, even on the hottest Louisiana afternoons. After being poured into the indoor bucket, we'd take turns sipping it with a shared dipper, a simple tin ladle that hung on a nail nearby. We all drank from it, children, grown folks, and elders alike: one dipper, one family. I can still picture Papa bringing that dipper to his mouth, pausing just before that first sip. As he tilted it back, his eyes would close just a little, and after that first swallow, his whole face would soften, almost like he had taken in peace itself. He'd let out a deep grunt of satisfaction, the kind that came not from being full but from being refreshed. That well water moved through the body like a blessing, you could feel it tracing its way from your lips to your chest, all the way down to the pit of your stomach, like a cool stream flowing deep through a forest path.

Back then, modern refrigeration didn't exist in our world, not in the way folks know it today. Keeping anything cool required planning and ingenuity. Instead of electric refrigerators, we had what was known as an icebox, a wooden chest lined with metal that relied on a block of ice to chill its contents. On Fridays, the iceman would come rolling down the road, usually once a week. He'd carry massive blocks of ice with iron tongs and deliver them house by house. Families could purchase twenty-five to fifty pounds of ice, depending on how much they could afford. We'd take that ice and set it on the top shelf of the icebox. Fresh produce and perishable items were stored underneath, where the melting block would keep them cool for two to three days, maybe a little longer if we were lucky and the weather cooperated. It was a delicate system, one that required coordination and care. But it worked. And in that wooden box, besides whatever scraps we had saved, was proof that we could preserve not just food but dignity, by making the most out of what little we had.

The food supply in our household didn't come from grocery store shelves, it came from the soil under our feet and the sweat of our Papa's brow. We were deeply connected to the land, not by choice but by necessity, and Papa's Garden was the heartbeat of that connection. He grew sweet potatoes, Irish potatoes, mustard greens, turnip greens, and black-eyed peas with care that bordered on reverence. He didn't farm for profit, he farmed for survival. For us. Rows of okra plants stood tall and proud like green pillars of resilience, their pods sliced and dropped into iron pots of soup or fried in cornmeal. Trips to the store were rare and specific, we only bought what we couldn't grow ourselves: sugar, flour, coffee, and sometimes meat. But for everything else, we pulled it straight from the dirt, washed it in a bucket, and cooked it over fire. Life was more complicated in many ways, but it was simpler and far more sustainable. We didn't worry about grocery bills or packaging. We knew where every bite came from, because we had planted it, harvested it, or raised it with our own hands.

When the cold winds of winter set in, Papa would select one of his pigs and begin the butchering process, an annual ritual that felt almost sacred. He would kill the hog, cure the meat, and smoke it in the smokehouse that sat just behind the house like a quiet guardian. That process, salting and hanging the meat, letting it soak up smoke from hickory or oak, was both science and art. The curing added flavor, yes, but it also served a more practical purpose: it protected the meat, made it last, and kept it safe from bacteria and decay in a world without refrigeration. That smoked pork, hams shoulders, ribs, and fatback, would feed us for weeks, sometimes months. And we didn't waste anything. Even the bones found their way into pots of beans. Nothing was thrown away. Everything had a purpose.

But our way of life was more than just practical, it was a quiet, deliberate form of resistance. In a world that was designed to keep us dependent and disenfranchised, our ability to feed ourselves, raise our own meat, and rely on family was a radical act. We weren't looking for White-owned stores that didn't want our business or banks that refused us loans. We weren't waiting for handouts that never came. Instead, we turned to each other, to the land that had once been denied to us, and to the generational wisdom passed down from enslaved ancestors who had survived with even less. Our gardens weren't just about food, they were proof that we could provide for ourselves. Our smokehouses weren't just for meat, they were monuments to our endurance. Each seed planted was a declaration. Each harvest was an act of defiance. Every meal served at our table was a reminder that we may have been denied equality, but we would never be denied our dignity.

The atmosphere in our little community was warm and interwoven. We didn't have much, but we had each other, and that meant more than anything money could buy. Everyone looked out for one another. A neighbor's child was your child. If someone was sick, someone else brought broth. If wood needed chopping, someone came with an axe. There was one doctor in the area, but visits to him were rare in our household. Doctors were for emergencies, for people with money, or for situations when a baby was coming, and complications were feared. Most of the time, women gave birth right there at home, under the careful hands of a midwife, and I was no exception. A midwife brought me into the world, just as she had countless others. I can faintly remember my older brother going to the doctor once or twice, though the reason must've been serious because it wasn't something you did casually. Medical care was a privilege, something you hoped you didn't need. I didn't get the chance to step foot in a doctor's office until I joined the Army. By then, I had already learned how to live without it. In our world, healing often comes from prayer, poultice, and patience, and most of all, from people who love you enough to sit by your side and see you through.

When someone in our community got sick, we didn't reach for the telephone to call a doctor, we called on the elders. In our world, healing was communal, passed down through stories, recipes, and touch. During my childhood, when a fever wouldn't break or a cough lingered too long, we'd seek out a lady known to everyone as Elizbeth Casey, known to me as Aunt Liz. Aunt Liz wasn't just a neighborhood helper, she was our healer, our unofficial nurse, our medicine woman. She was a fair-skinned lady with long, curly black hair and an aura that made children both curious and cautious. She moved with quiet confidence, always wearing a long dress and carrying a basket that might as well have been a magic satchel. She had a remedy for every ailment, and somehow, her hands always knew where the pain was before you could even describe it.

Her knowledge had been passed down from her grandmother, and she treated it like a sacred heritage. Aunt Liz made concoctions and poultices from roots, herbs, oils, and whatever else the land would offer. Honey to heal a wound. Cherries steeped in water for gout. And the dreaded cod liver oil, bitter and thick, poured onto a spoon and forced down our throats with the promise that it would "keep our eyes bright." We didn't like it. We'd squirm and protest. But we took it anyway because Aunt Liz said so, and in those days, that was enough. She swore by those remedies, and funny enough, science is only now catching up to the wisdom she lived by. Long before pharmacies and health food stores praised natural medicine, Aunt Liz was already using what God had grown. And it worked.

The cold winters and hot summers were the lifestyle of the people in the countryside, and we made peace with both. Life wasn't always easy, it had its ups and downs, but I can honestly say that during those years living at Papa's house, I didn't feel like I was missing out on anything. I wasn't trapped in fear. I wasn't weighed down by city noise or burdened by what we didn't have. What I did have was time with my family, working beside them, laughing with them, and learning what it meant to live in rhythm with the land. There was always something to do, gardening, hauling wood, drawing water, but there was joy in it, too. There was a peace that hung in the air, a kind of freedom that didn't depend on money or permission. We all knew each other. We lived as a community. Our doors weren't locked, and our fears were few. Those were the good old days, not because life was perfect, but because we were present in it. And even now, after all these years, I don't think I've ever felt the same security, peace, and belonging that I felt back then, under Papa's roof, surrounded by love, warmed by the fire, and held by everything that mattered.

Two years after moving back to my grandfather's house in Loggy Bayou, we faced a loss that would change everything. On May 23, 1939, my grandmother, Clifford Daniels, passed away inside that very house, the same house where she had raised eleven children and welcomed countless grandchildren. She died quietly in one of the back bedrooms, her life drawing to a close like the final verse of a well-loved hymn. It was a peaceful passing, but it left a silence that felt heavy and permanent. The house, large and lived-in, had a wide hallway running down the center like a river, and her room was tucked to the left, right across from my mother's. I remember the air that day, it wasn't just hot with the early Louisiana summer, it was thick with grief and waiting.

People moved like they were underwater. Some cried softly, others prayed in whispers. She didn't die in a hospital surrounded by machines. She died at home, surrounded by love and legacy, the voices of her people carrying her into eternity.

It was May, and the heat had already settled in like a blanket over the land. They placed her body on a cooling board, a flat wooden surface used before funeral homes became the norm and kept her in the room overnight. The adults used whatever they could, embalming fluid, blocks of ice, water-soaked sheets, to slow time until the funeral could be held. That night, the house was overtaken by a strange mixture of chemical sharpness and sorrow, the scent of preservation mingling with the quiet cries of women who had once leaned on her strength. As children, we were not ushered away. We were expected to witness, to absorb, to learn. Death was not hidden from us, it was part of the rhythm of life. When she was finally buried the next day, the women went to work, scrubbing the room from top to bottom, wiping down the walls, the floors, and the linens. But no matter how hard they cleaned, the scent of loss clung to the space. And deep in the walls, I think the memory stayed.

My grandfather was never quite the same. That first night after the funeral, the grandchildren gathered in the hallway, sensing something had shifted. One of the adults asked who would sleep with Papa that night so he wouldn't be alone. Without hesitation, he said, "I want Roy." I was just a boy, maybe ten years old, but I was chosen. I didn't want to do it, not really. I had heard all kinds of tales about spirits and ghosts slapping children in the night, stories passed down like scripture. They said haints rode the wind, crept through cracks, and slapped you awake just to let you know that the veil between the worlds was thin. Grown folks swore you could smell them in the room before you saw them, that they'd chill the air and whisper in corners. Papa would sometimes sit on the porch at night and say he heard them rustling through the trees or climbing up the side of the house. He once sent me out in the rain, claiming he could hear the haints moving and needed me to draw water from the well to ward them off. That fear was alive in me as I stood there, a little boy called into a grief too big for his shoulders. I didn't want to lie next to a man full of sorrow in the same bed where love had just left its last breath. But I didn't protest. In those days, children didn't say no. I crawled into bed behind him, stiff as a board, my body trembling with every creak in the house. The smell of liniment and sadness filled my nose. I stared at the ceiling, afraid to blink, fearful of what might be watching in the dark. And still, I stayed. I stayed because I was asked to. I stayed because I was needed. That moment, being called to stand in, to be a small comfort to a man who had lost his life's companion, planted something in me. I didn't know it then, but it was the beginning of a lifelong lesson. That night, something passed between us, not in words but in silence. In stillness. In presence. That was the beginning of me learning what it meant to carry burdens, not because I was strong but because someone had to. It was the beginning of understanding that fear does not excuse you from responsibility. That sometimes, to serve, to love, to grow, you must lie down in your discomfort and keep breathing through it. Her death didn't just take something from us, it gave us something, too. It gave me a quiet understanding of what it meant to show up, even when you're scared, and it taught me that even grief can plant seeds.

After my grandmother died, the walls echoed differently. The meals were quieter. Papa sat a little more still. He didn't talk about her much after that, but you could feel the emptiness in his movements. The matriarch was gone, and with her went a kind of rhythm that had held everything together.

The years that followed were slow, quiet, and aching in their own way. Mama did what she could to keep the house in motion. Papa kept working the land, shoulders bent but spirit steady. Life went on because it had to, but something in all of us had shifted. Grief doesn't always wail; sometimes, it just hums beneath everything.

And yet, slowly, life began to stretch again. Babies were born. Crops were planted. The laughter started to return in small doses, at supper tables, on porches, and in the pews of Liberty Hill. And then came 1942.

That year, something rare happened. It is the kind of thing you don't plan but feel in your bones. All of Papa's children came home. Not for a funeral. Not because someone had passed. But because they wanted to. Because it was time. They called it "Papa Day," though I don't know who named it first. It wasn't a holiday, but it felt holy, a day to honor the quiet man who had raised them all with steady hands and little fanfare.

And for once, just once, we were whole again.

Before the fractures. Before the silence. Before the turkey drama and funeral tears, there was one golden day when everything and everyone came together.

I was just a little boy, legs still skinny, fists still soft, ears tuned to the rhythms of grown folks' laughter and the gospel melodies of Liberty Hill. Papa, Alfred Daniels, was the center of our family tree, and on that day, every branch bent back home. His children came from every corner of the state, maybe beyond. The yard filled with cousins I didn't even know I had. The house buzzed with stories, with shouting, with singing. It was the kind of gathering that didn't happen often, but when it did, you could feel the Spirit pressing close.

We held it at Papa's house. The dirt yard was swept clean, and long folding tables were covered in oilcloth. Dishes were piled high. Chicken was fried in cast iron. Cornbread was hot from the pan. Mason jars clinked like music. You could hear the sound of living, good, rich, full-bodied living, in every direction.

But what I remember most, the part etched into my memory like a scar and a smile, was when they made me box Baby Dear, one of my younger cousins. The grown folks formed a ring right there in the yard, laughing and egging us on like it was Madison Square Garden. Baby Dear had quick hands. I had great pride. I don't remember who won, but I do remember my feelings being more bruised than my body. They laughed, but I felt like crying. Not from the hit, but from the moment, from being on display.

Still, that was the kind of memory you carry with you, not because it was easy but because it was whole.

That day was a snapshot of something we would never fully reclaim. We didn't call it Grandfather's Day back then. It wasn't official. But to us, it meant something. It was a tribute in its most valid form: food, family, presence, a living thank-you. Papa sat in the shade that day, smiling, quiet, proud. The man who had raised his children on sweat land and dignity now watched his grandchildren chase chickens and each other through that red clay yard. It was unity before the unraveling.

Years later, when I watched the family fracture over carving rights and funeral tension, I'd think back to Papa Day. To the sound of screen doors swinging. To the smell of neck bones and onions. To that one round of backyard boxing that made me feel both small and seen.

That was the last time, before the war, before migration, before loss and pride and time did their work, that we were all just one big family under one roof. And I've held onto that day ever since.

LIBERTY HILL

But while the grown folks were gathering, grieving, and building lives, I was just beginning to shape my own. In those same years, quietly, steadily, another kind of foundation was being laid beneath my feet, not with cement or wood, but with words, numbers, memory, and song.

It started at Liberty Hill. In the early 1940s, around the same time as Papa Day, deep in the Jim Crow South, I began my formal education at Liberty Hill, a place that wore two hats with equal reverence. During the week, it was our schoolhouse, filled with desks, blackboards, and hand-me-down books from the White schools in town. But come Sunday, those same wooden floors held the sacred hush of worship. The chalkboard gave way to a pulpit, and students became congregants. There were no janitors to clean between functions, no fancy transitions, just a transformation born of necessity and faith. Liberty Hill was our classroom, our church, our training ground, and our altar.

That building wasn't just wood and nails, it was the soul of our community, a place where Black children learned their letters and their worth, where prayers were whispered over arithmetic, and where the dream of dignity was passed from one generation to the next.

School wasn't a given for us. It was a sacrifice. It meant waking up before dawn, walking miles barefoot down dusty roads, and sitting in cold, drafty rooms with nothing but a potbelly stove and prayer to keep us warm. We had about thirty-five children in our schoolhouse, all jammed into one room, covering grades one through seven. There were no grade-specific classes and no neatly organized rows of desks. You learned what you could when you could, sometimes from the teacher and sometimes from a student just one step ahead of you.

And those teachers? Most of them were barely older than us. After finishing eleventh grade, the highest many could go, they were sent right back to the community to teach. No training. Just a blackboard, a box of chalk, and a calling. Still, they carried themselves with authority because they knew that what they were doing mattered.

Our books were hand-me-downs from the White schools. Torn covers. Missing pages. White children's names were scribbled out in the front and replaced with ours. Some books were so used up that they were more tape than paper. But we made do. We were used to secondhand things, secondhand desks, secondhand supplies, secondhand chances. We didn't complain. We didn't know we were supposed to.

Learning felt like survival. We leaned on each other. Older kids helped the younger ones sound out words, shared pencils, or repeated spelling lists out loud until the room was echoing with effort. I remember one time, my classmate Mable read a Bible verse so strong it hushed the room. That moment taught me: your voice can carry power, even if your pages are torn.

Liberty Hill had no electricity. Our only light came through tall, narrow windows or, if it was too dark, from the flicker of kerosene lamps. When winter came, the cold crept in under the doors and stayed in the corners. We'd huddle near the stove, rubbing our hands together between lessons. In those moments, we weren't just students. We were survivors. Would you believe I eventually became a schoolteacher, and earned a master's degree from Louisiana State University, and still didn't know about the Tulsa Race Massacre until just about ten years ago? That entire chapter of our history was kept from us. It wasn't in the books. It wasn't in the lessons. It wasn't even whispered. And I'm not alone. That kind of erasure was intentional. They didn't just want to hide the truth, they tried to shape our reality.

So, we grew up knowing just enough to stay in our place, but not enough to change it. That's what school was supposed to do: keep us content. But somehow, Liberty Hill did something else for me. It made me hungry to know more. It taught me how to learn with almost nothing. And that kind of learning? It sticks with you.

Still, life outside the classroom reminded us of who we were in the system's eyes. Every April, when the lessons were beginning to sink in, school would end, not for summer break, but for work; it was called cotton season. Our little Black school was dismissed a whole month before the White schools. Not because we were ahead. Not because we had finished. But because White cotton farmers needed us back in the fields. While White children kept learning in air-cooled classrooms, we were bent over in the heat, chopping and picking cotton with blistered fingers and sore legs.

I never forgot that. I still haven't. That's how the system was built: take our minds in the morning and our bodies in the afternoon. If we were lucky, we got leftovers. But we learned anyway. We dreamed anyway, even with all the odds stacked against us.

I remember sitting by the fire in Papa's house, my schoolbook on my lap, the pages warmed by the chimney glow. My fingers would trace the words, my lips whispering verses and passages we'd practiced in school. Mama said if I could read the Bible out loud without stumbling, I'd always find my way. And she was right.

Liberty Hill School didn't just teach me facts. It taught me resilience. It taught me the power of showing up, standing tall with bent knees, and learning even when the world told you weren't supposed to. That little schoolhouse, with its broken windows and borrowed books, helped make me who I am. It wasn't perfect. It wasn't fair. But it was sacred.

HARD LESSONS: UNCLE LUKE

AND THE WORK OF BOYS

After school let out in the spring, when cotton season called us out of classrooms and into the fields, I went to live with my mother's younger brother, Uncle Luke. He lived about seven miles from us, but his presence felt much closer. Uncle Luke was the kind of man whose name got ahead of him, rough-edged, sharp-tongued, and full of contradictions. He had a reputation you didn't forget, and time under his roof taught me lessons no school ever could.

Back then, folks gave Uncle Luke a nickname that wouldn't sit right today. It wasn't meant kindly and played on old stereotypes about money. They called him "Jew" not because of religion or background, he wasn't Jewish, but because he held on to a dollar like it was glued to his palm. That was the kind of talk people used in those days, rough, unfiltered, and often shaped by ignorance more than malice. Still, I'll say Uncle Luke was the stingiest man I ever met.

I didn't live with him long, but my time there left an imprint. Every Saturday, we'd go into town. Store to store, house to house, no real plan, just following his rhythm. He never bought me anything. Not a soda. Not a piece of candy. Not even a handful of peanuts from the country store. I'd trail behind him, watching how he moved, who he talked to, and how he worked every angle. Looking back now, I suspect he was involved in some dealings I had no business being nearby. There were moments I wondered if he was trying to teach me to steal, or at least, to see how far I'd bend. But I never did. Not once. I was raised under my mama's roof, which meant something.

Church school, Bible verses, decency. I may not have had much, but I had values. And in a world that tried to take everything from you, your values were something you could keep.

His wife, Aunt Bob, wasn't mean, but she sure knew how to run a boy like me. "Roy, fetch me a bucket of water." "Roy, sweep off the back porch." "Roy, bring in that firewood." It didn't matter that she had sons of her own, boys right around my age. She'd walk right past them and call my name. At first, I thought she trusted me more. Then I realized I was just the easiest to ask, quiet, respectful, and taught never to talk back.

It wasn't just the labor that wore me down, it was its lopsidedness. I'd be hauling in sacks of corn or dragging bundles of firewood while her sons leaned back in their chairs, chewing sugarcane and watching me sweat like the evening show. I remember one day, I slipped down in the chicken yard carrying a slop bucket, and they burst into laughter like it was the best thing they'd seen all week. Not one hand reached out. Not one voice offered help. That kind of silence, that smug detachment, did something to me. It made the work heavier. Not just because I was tired but because I was invisible. That's the kind of weight a boy remembers.

After enough long days of thankless work, I had enough. One day, she sent me to draw water again. I walked to the well, dropped the bucket, pulled it up, and carried it back with my arms shaking from the weight. When I stepped into that shotgun house, sweaty, tired, and tired of being tired, I flung that bucket of water right down the hallway. It splashed against the walls, soaked the floor, and sent everyone scrambling. I didn't say a word. I just walked away. And from that day on, Aunt Bob never bothered me again.

But my work didn't end there. Uncle Luke had a big red mule named Red. Before him, there was Nick, a smaller mule that was slow but manageable. I learned to plow with Nick, and once Uncle Luke saw I could handle it, he gave me Red, the strong one, the stubborn one. Red was a different kind of teacher. That mule didn't care about fairness or feelings. He didn't care if you were tired or if your hands were raw. He just knew the row had to be pulled, and if you didn't guide him right, he'd show you who really ran the field. But I grew to respect him. Red didn't talk behind your back. Red didn't make you beg. He just did what he was made to do and expected the same of me. I started learning more than just farming behind that mule. I learned rhythm. I learned discipline. I learned how to move forward even when everything in you wants to stop. That mule didn't just pull the plow, he pulled a boy into manhood.

Then, Uncle Luke just stopped showing up. He left me to run his place with no instruction, no help: just me, a mule, and a field. Every morning, I'd strap on that plow, walk behind Red, and drag the earth open like it was my job to wake it up. Dust in my nose. Sweat in my eyes. I learned how to read the soil, how it changed after rain, how to spot good rows, how to listen when the mule was about to break stubborn. I fed chickens, cleaned out pens, and mended fences. I worked through muscle pain, heat waves, and loneliness. And I did it all while his three sons sat idle.

Years later, when Uncle Luke, Aunt Bob, and their three sons were all dead and gone, and I was still standing, I passed by Uncle Luke's old place. The roof was sagging. The fields were wild again. I sat in my truck and just looked.

I thought about all the sweat I poured into that dirt. All the days I gave. All the things I carried. And how, somehow, I didn't come away bitter, I came away stronger. Maybe Uncle Luke knew what he was doing. Maybe he didn't. But I do know this: he helped make me. And for that, I can say thank you, even if he never did.

MISS MISS AND THE QUILT THAT
COULDN'T COVER ME

When my time at Liberty Hill ended, it wasn't because I had finished all my schooling, it was because the system had drawn a line I couldn't cross. After Liberty Hill, the next step was Ringgold Colored High School. But the parish bus didn't come all the way out to Loggy Bayou. If you couldn't get to school by yourself, you didn't go. It's as simple as that. And just like that, my education could've ended right there on the edge of the woods, not for lack of will, but for lack of wheels.

But Mama had other plans. She made a quiet, courageous decision that would change everything. She sent me to Shreveport to continue my education at Central Colored School. That decision wasn't easy. It wasn't fancy. But it was forward-thinking.

I went to live with her best friend, the woman everyone called Miss Miss. Her name was Minnie Allen, but nobody dared call her that. To us, she was Miss Miss, a sharp-tongued, straight-backed woman with no time for foolishness and no tolerance for laziness. She didn't pamper you, but she protected you. She loved with her actions, not her words. And under her roof, I learned that the world was bigger than Liberty Hill, and more complicated too.

Miss Miss lived in a small, worn-down house on a dusty street where time seemed to move like syrup, slow, thick, and heavy. The air smelled of sweat, red clay, and cooking grease, a constant reminder that life there was about survival, not comfort. The front porch sagged under the weight of years and footsteps, and the screen door creaked and snapped like it had its own opinion about every person who walked through it. That house didn't have much, but it had heart and hardship, in equal measure.

Inside, my world was stripped down to the barest essentials. I slept on the floor with nothing but a thin quilt and a lumpy pillow, laying out like an old dog's corner next to a wood-burning stove that could barely hold back the cold. There was no bed, no running water, and no refrigerator, nothing to keep food cold or preserve anything beyond a day or two. At night, a weak light bulb dangled from the ceiling, casting long, swaying shadows across the cracked walls. That little glow made the darkness seem deeper, the cold feel sharper. It wasn't just a place to stay, it was a lesson in what it meant to endure.

Behind the house, way out near the tree line, stood an old wooden outhouse, no plumbing, no light, just a hole in the ground beneath a weathered seat and a crescent moon carved into the door. It was shared by nearly everyone on the block, and when nature called, that's where you went, rain, shine, day, or night. Only two or three homes on the block owned its own outhouse, and none were anything to be proud of. That year, I did everything I could to avoid using it. I held everything in, waiting until I got to school the next day, where the toilets, though hardly sanitary, felt like a luxury in comparison. But truth be told, most nights, I didn't even need to go. There wasn't much food in my belly to move anything through.

When winter arrived, it didn't knock, it crept in, crawling up through the cracks in the floorboards, wrapping itself around your legs like an unwelcome guest. That quilt barely covered me. If I pulled it up to my shoulders, my feet stuck out, aching from the exposure. If I tucked in my feet, my chest shivered through the night. There was no winning. Most mornings, I woke with my feet raw and burning, like they'd spent the night walking through ice. I'd sit there, shivering in the dim gray light, reaching for one set of clothes I owned, stiff with cold and wear, pulling them on like armor for another day.

Yes, I wore the same outfit every day. Not because I was stubborn but because that's all I had. There are no choices to make, no colors to match, and no variety. I cleaned the same patched shirt and threadbare pants as best I could. I made sure they were neat. I made sure they were presentable. Because even when you have nothing, you carry yourself with dignity. That outfit became part of who I was, quiet, steady, unnoticed, but holding my head up all the same. I walked into school like I belonged there, even when I felt like I didn't.

School was my refuge. It was the one place where I didn't feel like I had to explain my poverty, where I wasn't defined by the floor I slept on or the quilt that barely covered me. There, amid chalk dust, wooden desks, and thin notebooks, God began to show me something. He began to reveal that favor could still grow even in the poorest soil. One of the people who saw something in me before I saw it in myself was Miss Brown, the principal's wife, and our science teacher. She wasn't just a teacher, she was a quiet builder of confidence. She would send me on small errands, trust me with responsibilities, call me to help pass out materials, and speak to me as if I mattered. Then, one day, out of nowhere, she made me the president of the class. Imagine a boy with nothing but one set of clothes, sleeping on a hard floor beside a dying fire, suddenly given the title of leadership. I didn't understand it then. But now, I know exactly what it was, God's hand of grace, showing me that I didn't have to look like success to be called to it.

By the time I was twelve or thirteen, most boys my age were already working at the Salt Mill, at the plant, wherever a few coins could be earned. They had money in their pockets, enough to take girls to the picture show, buy a bottle of soda, or treat themselves to something sweet. Not me. I was stuck between two worlds: too young to work, and too poor to play. But I didn't let that break me. I stayed focused. I kept studying, kept reading, and praying. My mother had sent me to Shreveport for a reason, to rise above. And even back then, when I didn't know much, I knew her sacrifice deserved my determination.

Sometimes in the evenings, after a long, cold day, I'd lie there on that hardwood floor, wrapped in my little quilt, listening to the wind rattle the bones of that old house. The walls would creak with age, and the shadows would stretch long across the room. I'd close my eyes and imagine what it might feel like to have a real bed. A mattress soft enough to sink into. A heavy blanket pulled up to my chin. A pillow that didn't go flat under my head. I wondered what it would be like to wake up warm for once. I wondered what it would feel like to open a closet full of clean shirts and pants, to have choices instead of just one set of clothes folded at the edge of the room like a reminder. But I didn't let myself dream for too long. Because hope, tender, fragile, and too large for that space, might have broken me back then, but I couldn't afford to break. So, instead, I endured. Quietly. Consistently. Day after day, I endured.

That year shaped me in ways that no classroom ever could. It taught me how to be tough when no one was watching, how to hold onto pride without needing applause, and how to carry weight in silence, with dignity that didn't come from clothes or comforts but from character. I learned that life doesn't hand you softness, it hands you struggle. And out of that struggle, if you don't give in, it forges you like iron through fire.

It was during that season that the nickname "Professor" finally stuck. My mama had called me that since I was little, half as a joke, half as a prophecy. Then my Aunt Doris picked it up, and before long, folks around Ringgold called me "Fess." It wasn't just a name, it was an identity, a signal that even though I had nothing, I carried wisdom beyond my years and a future bigger than anyone expected from a boy sleeping on the floor.

Years later, I would walk across Army bases, down the sidewalks of California, through the halls of Grambling, and into classrooms, pulpits, and a life richer than anything that cold little house in Shreveport ever promised. But the man I became, the teacher, the husband, the father, the preacher, was first formed right there. On that floor. In that house. Wrapped in a threadbare quilt, held together by grit, faith, and something God was already building inside of me.

And now, looking back with clearer eyes and a steadier heart, I understand what I didn't know then: Sometimes, the greatest blessings are born in the hardest places. Not in comfort, but in cold. Not in abundance, but in lack. Because it's there, in the dark, silence, and struggle, that God lays a foundation too strong for any storm to shake.

BACK TO RINGGOLD

After two long, hard years in Shreveport with Miss Miss, Minnie Allen, it was finally time for me to come home. I had survived those years sleeping on the floor each night with nothing but a thin quilt and a lumpy pillow, dodging cold drafts and pushing through hunger pains, holding fast to the small pieces of dignity a boy could gather when life stripped everything else away. I had made it through eighth and ninth grade, not by ease but by endurance. And now, Mama had called me back home.

I returned to Ringgold around 1947, and when I stepped off that bus, it felt like slipping into an old, threadbare coat, worn, familiar, and comforting in a way that only home can be. The air wrapped around me differently than it had in the city. It was thicker, earthier, and full of memory. It smelled like red clay dirt, pine sap, and woodsmoke curling from kitchen chimneys. The cicadas still sang their wild, rhythmic songs at dusk, and the porch screens still creaked in the heat like old voices whispering family stories. The old oak trees still stretched wide as if watching over us. Ringgold hadn't changed much, but I had.

I had learned how to live without comfort, how to move through hunger without complaint, and how to make something out of nothing. I didn't walk the same. I didn't talk the same. Something inside me had gone quiet, but it wasn't weakness. It was watchfulness. A sense of how the world worked and how I had to walk through it if I wanted to last.

The South was holding its breath in those days, caught in a tension between the old ways and the first tremors of something new. World War II had ended just two years before, in 1945, and soldiers, Black and White alike, had come home expecting that their sacrifices would finally mean something. That the world they had fought to save would now make room for them in it. President Truman had signed an executive order to desegregate the military in

1948, signaling that maybe the tide was beginning to turn. Jackie Robinson had already broken the color barrier in Major League Baseball in 1947, stepping onto the field not just as an athlete but as a symbol. A hero to Black boys like me, proving that we could stand tall on any field.

But down here in Ringgold, Louisiana, the signs of progress didn't reach quite so far. Jim Crow was still the law, and the weight of it pressed against our necks daily. Signs still told us where we could and couldn't sit, eat, drink, or even pray. Black families still lived under the unspoken threat of violence, lynchings, night riders, and unanswered crimes. We still picked cotton for pennies, and we still knew to lower our eyes and speak softly when a White man was near. Justice didn't wear a badge for us. It wore a rope. And we learned early: silence was survival.

Coming home meant stepping back into all of that, into a world where Black life was boxed in by boundaries others had drawn. But it also meant stepping into something steady.

Here, at least, I had my people. I had the land beneath my feet that knew my name. I had elders who prayed over me, neighbors who watched out for me, and a mother who had waited for my return. And there's a particular kind of strength in that, a strength that doesn't come from freedom but from familiarity, from roots that run deep and wide, even in unforgiving soil.

When I enrolled at Ringgold Colored High School, I wasn't a boy anymore. Hardship had carved me down to something leaner, sharper. I had made it through Shreveport, sleeping on floors, living off little, and learning how to carry myself when I didn't even have proper shoes on my feet. By the time I returned, I was taller and quieter, my clothes were worn thin, and my back was straighter. My spirit had been stitched up by survival, and it showed.

High school felt like a different world. The halls were rough, the textbooks ragged, and the teachers a mixed bag of intention. Some were kind. Some weren't. I'll never forget

Miss James, my English teacher. She had a way of making even the poorest student feel seen, she never raised her voice but could silence a room with a single look. She treated us like we had minds worth sharpening. Then there were others who didn't bother to learn our names, who stood in front of the class but never looked us in the eye, teachers who saw us as statistics, not students. One or two, I'm sure, wondered if we were even worth the effort.

But I showed up. I wasn't at the top of the class, but I wasn't a fool either. I had learned by then that success wasn't always about being the smartest, it was about being the most determined. And that was something I carried in spades.

Student life was sparse. There weren't many clubs or organized activities for us Black kids, not the way there were for the White students across town. But we made our own fun, our own pride. We had pep rallies, even if we didn't have band uniforms or brand-new pom-poms. We had homecoming events, even if our decorations were made from scrap paper, and shared hope. And we had the gym, the same gym where I would one day graduate. It was small, hot in the summer, cold in the winter, but it was ours.

I remember the way the bell rang loud and sharp, echoing through the cinder block hallways. I remember the dusty windows, the smell of chalk, and the way the sun would spill across the floor during morning announcements. I remember laughing too loud with the boys in the back of the room, even when we had nothing to laugh about. It was those small, defiant moments of joy that kept us going. Because when the system tries to break you, smiling becomes a form of rebellion.

We country boys were often looked down on by the town kids, who called us "Lake Cooters." It was meant as an insult, a way to say we were backward, unsophisticated, and a little too country for the classroom. Maybe we were. We wore secondhand clothes, came in with red dust on our shoes, and talked slower than the city kids. But what we lacked in polish, we made up for in heart. We had grit. We had manners. We had mothers who told us to stand tall and not let anybody shame us for where we came from. So when they called us Lake Cooters, we let them. And then we outworked them. Quietly. And by the time graduation rolled around, some of those same boys were following my lead.

At school assemblies, we'd sit in long rows on wooden benches, listening to teachers speak about respect, about rising above. Sometimes, we'd sing hymns, voices cracking but trying. It wasn't about show, it was about staying rooted in something bigger than textbooks. I still remember the weight of those gym bleachers and the sound of our shoes tapping the floor while we waited for our names to be called in honor roll or spelling bee rounds. There were few frills, but there was pride in every small moment.

Outside of school, life didn't get any easier. I still had to pick cotton, chop wood, and haul water in a five-gallon bucket that slapped against my leg with every step. I still rose before the rooster and worked until the sun dipped behind the trees. But even with all the labor and weariness, there was one thing that gave me a momentary taste of freedom: swimming.

After spending long hours behind a mule, dragging a plow through dry earth, sweat soaking through my clothes, and dirt crusted on my neck, nothing felt better than slipping into the calm waters of the nearby pond. It wasn't much, a muddy stretch of still water surrounded by thick brushes and shaded trees, but to us boys, it was paradise. That pond didn't care how poor we were, how sunburned our backs had gotten, or how many chores we still had waiting. It accepted us just as we were. For a little while, we could be boys again, splashing and laughing, floating on our backs, and watching the sky stretch out above us. No adults barking orders. No chores. No switches. Just water, wind, and the kind of joy that can't be bought.

We would run barefoot down the path; shirts balled up in our fists, hearts light with mischief and freedom. That pond washed the weight off our shoulders. And even though I was supposed to be helping on the farm or tending to chores, I would steal away whenever I could. Just a quick dip. Just a moment to breathe.

But Mama didn't like it. Not one bit. She had her reasons, and they were carved from experience and fear. She would warn me again and again, her voice edged with urgency: "Don't go swimming down there with those White boys. If something happens to one of them, they'll blame you." She wasn't guessing. She was remembering. Back then, all it took was proximity. If a White child got a cramp, slipped underwater, or so much as scraped a knee, and you were nearby, you were guilty. No trial, no questions, no second chances. A Black boy didn't need to do anything wrong to be punished. He just had to be present.

But I was young. I didn't understand the danger the way she did. I thought I was careful. I thought I could sneak off, take a quick swim, and come home the long way around. The pond was only a quarter mile from the house, and for a little while, I thought I was getting away with it. I'd dry off behind the trees, shake the mud from my legs, and walk the back road with my heart still beating fast from the fun.

Then, one day, I came up from the water smiling, the sun warm on my skin, the laughter of the boys still echoing around me, and I saw her. Mama.

She was standing on top of my clothes, arms crossed, her mouth set in a way that told me it was too late for any explanation. In one hand, she held a switch, not the thick kind that bruised, but the thin, flexible one that whistled when it cut through the air. She didn't yell. She didn't raise her voice. She didn't even move right away. She just stood there, still as stone, letting the silence speak.

I tried to gather my words and plead with her, but none of it mattered. That walk home was one I'd never forget. Every step marked by the sting of that switch, every swing echoed her fear more than her anger. She didn't whip me because I disobeyed. She whipped me because I had risked everything. Because I had stepped into a space where a simple mistake, one I couldn't control, might have meant she would lose me forever.

Looking back now, I know that whipping was love in its most desperate form. It was protection in motion. She had already lost so much in her life, security, partnership, comfort, and the idea of losing one of her children to injustice was too much to bear. I didn't understand it then, but I do now.

To this day, whenever I see a swimming pool, especially one filled with White folks, something in me tightens. I pause. That memory rises up fresh as ever, the splash of water, the shock of seeing her standing there, the heat of shame on my face, and the sting of that switch along my back. I hear her voice even now, not in anger, but in fear. In truth.

She wasn't just trying to raise a son, she was trying to keep me alive in a world that had already made up its mind about boys who looked like me. That lesson stayed with me longer than any scar. It made me cautious. It made me aware. But more than that, it made me grateful.

Because even though I wanted to be free, I needed to survive. That pond taught me something school never could, that danger could find you even in the joy, that a Black boy's laughter could be mistaken for trouble. And that Mama's love was fierce because the world was fiercer still.

So when I lay down at night, now in a real bed, not a patch of floor, I didn't just dream of rest. I dreamed of escape. I dreamed of putting on a cap and gown. I dreamed of walking across a stage, and out of the shadows that Ringgold tried to cast over boys like me.

In 1950, I did just what I had dreamed about. I graduated from Ringgold Colored High School. There was no parade, no spotlight. Just a borrowed cap, a cheap gown, and my family sitting proud and quiet in the back row. I took that diploma in hand and knew exactly what it meant. It was my passport, out of the fields, out of poverty, out of the shadow of a world that had tried to define me.

It was a future forged in struggle and laced with hope. A future that would take me into the Army, into Grambling State University, into classrooms, pulpits, and communities where I would one day return the lessons I had learned. But it all started here. Back in Ringgold. The town that tried to hold me down but never could. I had outgrown its boundaries, even if my feet still walked its roads.

INTO THE ARMY

In 1950, with my diploma from Ringgold Colored High School tucked under my arm and a heart full of uncertainty, I stepped onto a path that would change my life forever. I hadn't planned on joining the United States Army. When school ended, the world beyond the cotton fields and dirt roads stretched wide like an open sky, full of possibility, yes, but also full of the unknown. All I knew for sure was how to work, how to chop cotton fast and clean, how to run behind a mule from sunup to sundown, how to press through the heat, the pain, and the monotony of life in the rural South. But beyond that, the future was still a blank page.

It was Mama who planted a different vision in my spirit. She had seen me by the glow of an oil lamp, bent over borrowed books after long days in the field, determined to carve something out of nothing. I remembered her calling me "Professor", not with surprise, but with certainty. She wasn't naming what I was. She was naming what I would become.

In our community, a name like that wasn't casual. It was a laying on of hands. It was her way of saying, "I see you. I believe in what you haven't even lived yet." That word wrapped itself around me like a mantle. It didn't make the journey easier, but it made the weight holy.

After graduation, I lingered at home, caught between the familiar and the unknown. I didn't know what came next. That's when my first cousin, Junior White, David White Jr., came all the way from California to get me. He was more than family; he was my guardian angel, my chariot sent by God when I didn't know how to move forward. We had graduated the same year, and he was determined that we were going into the Army together. He believed in the uniform. He believed in me. And maybe, just maybe, I needed someone to believe in me at that moment.

Now, my grandfather had always said I had flat feet, and for years, I thought that meant I wouldn't be accepted into the military. It wasn't so much a medical diagnosis as it was a family saying, his way of telling me I wasn't built for running off into things, that I was meant to stay grounded. "You ain't going in no Army," he'd say. "You got flat feet." And deep down, I believed him. So, when Junior White said we were headed to the recruiting station, I feared they'd turn me away. But I went anyway, half expecting rejection, fully prepared for it.

We made our way to the recruiting office in Texarkana, Texas, a busy, segregated town buzzing with soldiers, cotton workers, and the heavy smell of train smoke. It was a place where uniforms brushed past overalls, where pride and poverty existed side by side. The Army was eager for young Black men with high school diplomas, and they didn't ask too many questions. They housed us in a Black hotel in town and handed us meal tickets, and for two boys raised on farm food and hand-me-downs, it felt like we had stepped into a new world. We ate better than we ever had, slept on real mattresses, and it felt like the world might have room for us for a brief moment.

I wasn't afraid of the Army itself. What scared me was whether I'd even get the chance. But I passed the physical. No one said a word about flat feet. Maybe my Papa had been wrong. Or perhaps the Army just needed bodies too badly to care. Either way, I was in. We were sworn in, handed government-issued everything, and just like that, I was a soldier.

From there, we boarded a troop train heading north toward Fort Riley, Kansas, carrying our dreams, fears, and duffel bags. The rhythm of that train clacking against the rails sounded like change. And though I didn't know exactly where life was taking me, I knew I had made it. I had stepped into something my grandfather never thought I would, and I was determined to prove, to him, the world, and myself, that I belonged.

The South in 1950 was still bleeding, open wounds from slavery, from Reconstruction, from Jim Crow. You could feel it in the air, in the soil, in the way folks looked at you when you stepped out of line. Even though President Truman had ordered the desegregation of the military in 1948, down in Louisiana and across much of the country, segregation still strutted around like it owned the place. Paper laws didn't change hardened hearts overnight. And that prejudice ran deep, even inside the walls of the United States Army.

The train ride to Fort Riley, Kansas, was long and noisy. The car rocked from side to side as it chugged across miles of farmland, hissing and clanking over steel tracks. The smell of oil, coal, smoke, and metal clung to everything. I sat by the window, my hands resting on my knees, watching the fields roll by, wondering what was waiting on the other end of the line. I'd never been that far from home before, and while I didn't say it out loud, I carried a mix of fear and fire in my chest. I had made it out of Ringgold. Now, I had to make it through the Army.

Basic training began the moment our boots hit the dirt. The drill sergeants didn't care who you were, where you came from, or what you thought you knew. They barked orders like bullets, fast and sharp, and we learned to move fast, or pay for it. We ran. We marched. We learned how to stand still without blinking and how to fire everything from rifles and pistols to thirty-caliber machine guns. I remember the day they strapped one of those machine guns to my back and sent us marching eight miles under the Kansas sun, the heat pressing down like judgment. The sweat baked into your skin, dried in the folds of your uniform, and cracked you open from the inside out.

Some of the White boys fainted on that trail. I watched them stumble and drop, legs buckling like broken fence posts. The medics loaded them into ambulances, their chests heaving, faces pale. I remember thinking, "They ain't built for this."

I'll admit, once, I tried to fake a faint myself, to get a break. But I didn't know how to fall right. So, I kept marching.

The Army didn't know this: I had been in basic training my whole life. I had hauled 200-pound sacks of cotton across cracked earth, my feet slipping through dust and sweat. I chased cows barefoot through thorn bushes and mud. I had picked cotton under a sun just as hot as Kansas and had done it without water breaks or medics standing by. So no, hard work didn't scare me. Army training was just another field to cross.

We practiced low crawls under live machine gun fire, our bellies scraping against gravel while barbed wire snagged and tore at our shirts, and bullets hissed just inches overhead. Charges packed with high explosives detonated nearby, shaking the earth so violently it felt like the ground itself was trying to throw us off. The blasts came with a sudden, chest-thumping roar, followed by the sharp tang of burnt chemicals hanging in the air. There was no room for hesitation. You obeyed. You moved. You survived. And if you didn't, they made it plain, hesitation in war meant someone didn't go home.

At night, after chow, we'd scrape the mud from our boots, polish them till they shined, and sit rigid on bunks lined up like tombstones, waiting for the next order to be barked. Discipline soaked into our bones. Even now, after all these years, when someone of authority enters the room, my back still straightens on instinct, and my heels click together without a second thought. That's not just training, that's muscle memory forged in fire, discipline etched into the marrow.

But even in that discipline, I carried something more. I carried the lessons of my mother's voice, the weight of my grandfather's doubts, the prophecy of being called "Professor," and the strength of every hard day I'd already survived. I didn't just march in Kansas, I marched with the full weight of Louisiana behind me, determined to prove that a poor Black boy from Ringgold could go toe-to-toe with any man in uniform.

They kept us busy from sunup to lights out. There was no such thing as idle time in the Army. When we weren't out on the field crawling through barbed wire or firing downrange, we were back in the barracks or on KP duty, short for kitchen patrol. Every soldier had their turn. Once a week, I'd find myself in a steaming mess hall, peeling mountains of potatoes, scrubbing soot-blackened pots as big as bathtubs, and wiping down metal counters until they shone like new dimes. You'd be surprised how much discipline you can learn while elbow-deep in dishwater. The Army didn't just train your body, it trained your mindset. Even cleaning was part of the formation. You took pride in everything you did, even if no one else noticed.

If you were lucky, and stayed in line, you could earn a three-day pass from Friday night to Sunday evening. And on those weekends, we didn't waste a minute. We'd head to the day room, a big, echoing space with pool tables, table tennis, old radios, and wooden benches that creaked beneath our weight. It wasn't much, but it felt like freedom. For a few hours, we could laugh like boys again, cracking jokes, bragging about hometown girls, even forgetting, just for a little while, that war was looming.

Then, twelve grueling weeks later, basic training finally came to an end. We lined up one last time on the parade field, straight-backed and stone-faced, as names were read off and assignments handed out. I was sent to Fort Belvoir, Virginia, to train as a heavy equipment operator. The idea thrilled me. I might spend my Army days driving bulldozers, pushing earth, carving airstrips and roads through untamed landscapes, doing the kind of work that left a mark on the land. It seemed fitting, me, a boy raised behind a mule and plow, now operating machines that could move mountains. But the world had other plans.

The Korean War, which had already begun, was escalating fast. Political tension turned into troop deployments. What we thought would be training became preparation for combat. The Army needed boots on the ground more than it needed bulldozer operators. And just like that, the future I imagined, of working behind the wheel, steady and skilled, was swallowed by the needs of war.

I was shipped to Oakland, California, along with hundreds of other young soldiers, Black, White, nervous, excited, unsure. The base there was loud and sprawling, a place of transition where men moved like parts of a machine that never stopped grinding. After a few days of waiting, we were herded onto a creaking military transport ship, our names checked off one by one as we climbed the ramp with our duffel bags slung over our shoulders. None of us really knew where we were going. Orders were vague, as they often were. But once we were below deck and the steel door clanged shut behind us, it became clear: we were heading north. Far north.

The ocean crossing was brutal. The sea was cold and choppy, and the old transport ship, Andrew Jackson, groaned like it was trying to survive the journey with us. Men leaned over the rails, retching into the dark waters, their faces pale and drawn, the mess hall stank of sickness. You could be sitting there with a tray of powdered eggs and gray meat, and the man next to you would throw up right into his plate like it was nothing. We tried to ignore it, tried to eat through the waves of nausea, but the stench of vomit mixed with salt air clung to the walls, the floor, your clothes, your skin. It's a smell you don't forget. Not ever. That trip taught me something: you don't have to be in combat to suffer.

When we finally docked at Fort Richardson near Anchorage, the change in temperature slapped us hard. The cold wasn't just a chill, it was a presence. It bit through your uniform, through your boots, right into your bones.

I'd never felt the air so clean and so cruel at the same time. Snow sat heavy on the roofs of the buildings, and the trees were tall and still, like sentinels. It was beautiful and terrifying.

But we didn't stay long in Anchorage. From there, we were shipped out further, to the Aleutian Islands, a ragged chain of volcanic rock reaching westward like a finger pointed at Russia's icy doorstep. It felt like the edge of the world. Jagged cliffs dropped into a gray, endless sea. The wind never stopped. It screamed across the tundra, howling through the cracks in the windows, rattling the tin roofs of the barracks like they might peel away at any moment. The sun barely made an appearance, and when it did, it only highlighted how lonely the place truly was.

Eagles circled high overhead, their massive wings spread wide against the steel-colored sky, as if they were keeping watch over men far from home. And we were far, far from Louisiana, far from warmth, far from anything familiar. The isolation was thick, the kind that could sit on your chest and make it hard to breathe.

But just when we thought the cold had stripped all the joy out of life, we stumbled into a little unexpected fun, the kind you don't plan for, but remember forever.

Up in Alaska, where the wind cut through your bones and the snow never seemed to stop falling, the Postal Exchange, or the PE, as we called it, burned to the ground one winter. Nobody ever figured out how it caught fire, but what stuck with us wasn't the smoke, it was the beer. Somehow, by the grace of God or the stubbornness of Schlitz cans, the malt liquor survived, cases of it, buried in the snow behind the charred ruins, frozen but fully intact. For the next two months, we had ourselves a supply of free beer, cold and ready, no fridge needed. We'd go scratching through the snowbanks like kids on a treasure hunt, pulling out a can after can of Schlitz Malt Liquor and drinking it like we had just won the lottery. The officers didn't say a word. I figure they either didn't care or were quietly drinking it too. Either way, it was the best unofficial ration we ever had.

Our mission was salvage. After World War II, when the fighting stopped and the soldiers went home, the Army left behind mountains of equipment scattered across those islands, tanks, trucks, bulldozers, jeeps, generators, left to rust in the cold, forgotten by everyone except Uncle Sam. Our job was to find it, drag it out of snowdrifts and moss, clean it up, and ship it back to the mainland. We were like treasure hunters in a frozen graveyard.

One of the hardest things about Alaska wasn't the cold, it was the unpredictability. You never knew what the day would bring. We weren't on a battlefield, but the work still carried danger. Real danger. One wrong move on that frozen earth and someone could end up badly hurt, or worse.

I remember one day in particular. I was driving a bulldozer, the same as I had for weeks, clearing pathways through snow-packed tundra, pulling rusted-out vehicles from the old war sites. That day, one of the White soldiers had gotten his dozer stuck in a dip, the treads frozen into the earth like the ground was trying to swallow it whole. He waved me over, called for help, and I did what we all did up there, we worked together, race or no race. We weren't friends. We weren't enemies. We were just two men trying to get through the day.

We hooked the two bulldozers together, mine up front, his in the back. There was slack in the chain, and one of the sergeants, a guy I didn't know well but who'd always seemed sharp, stepped in to direct us. He motioned for me to back up slowly, and I did. But before I knew it, that slack snapped tight, and my machine jerked forward with all its weight. I didn't even see it happen, not really. One moment he was standing, the next he was down.

The cable had whipped tight, and the steel coupling caught him just wrong, sliced into his leg deep, like a blade made of iron and speed. Blood hit the snow like ink spilling on white paper. For a second, no one moved. Then everything was chaos. Men shouting. Radios crackling. Someone grabbed rags and tried to stop the bleeding. I stood frozen in the cab, hands locked on the controls, my breath fogging the glass. I couldn't believe it. One second, we were working, and the next, that man's future was bleeding out into the snow.

They rushed him to the airstrip and flew him out that same afternoon, flown straight to Walter Reed. That's all we heard. No letters. No word. Just gone.

He was White, and I was Black. But in that moment, none of that mattered. Pain doesn't care about color. Neither does regret. We were just two soldiers trying to do a job in a place that didn't forgive mistakes. And that day, something shifted in me. I realized how fragile life was, even off the battlefield. The uniform didn't make you invincible. The work didn't guarantee you'd go home whole. It could've been me.

But even out there, on the edge of the map, the Army's color line still held. Blacks on one side, Whites on the other.

Separate barracks. Separate mess tables. Separate everything. That line followed us across oceans, across landscapes, across every conversation. You could be sharing a snowstorm with a White soldier, standing side by side in freezing winds, but at night, you slept apart, you ate apart, you existed apart. That was just how it was.

Still, the cold had a way of leveling things. When the blizzards came, when the heaters in the barracks failed and the walls groaned under the weight of snow, a man was just a man. We shared blankets. We passed around cigarettes. We learned that frostbite doesn't care what color you are. Misery made us human again, if only for a night or two.

There were times I'd sit alone, looking out at the ocean, thinking about Ringgold, Mama, and the fields I used to walk barefoot. I'd wonder how I ended up in the middle of nowhere, on an island covered in rusted tanks and frozen silence. But I also knew that this was the path God had laid out for me. And I was learning. I was watching. I was being shaped.

Because even in Alaska, even in a place that tried to break you with cold and isolation, I carried something more substantial: the fire planted in me by struggle, and the knowledge that one day, I would return home with more than I left with. I would carry experience, discipline, and the beginning of purpose.

Later, after the long months spent in the frozen edges of the world, I was transferred to Fort Lewis, Washington. I remember stepping off that train and being struck by how different everything felt. The air was cool but not cruel, damp with the smell of moss and rainfall instead of snow and salt. The evergreens towered above the barracks like watchful giants. There was life in them, movement. It felt softer somehow, though I knew better than to let my guard down. And then, by some twist of fate, or grace, I received an unexpected assignment: the base pharmacy. When I arrived, I wasn't a trained medic and didn't know the difference between bandages and a dressing. But the Army didn't always have the luxury of formalities. They needed hands, and I had two steady ones. Under the watchful eye of a White doctor, a man who, in a time and place where respect between Black and White men was rare, chose to treat me with dignity, I began to learn. He didn't talk down to me. He explained things. He expected me to get it right. And I did.

I learned to fill prescriptions, carefully counting pills, measuring liquids, and labeling jars with clean handwriting. I was so quick at learning that I was able to write my first prescription on the first day. I helped treat minor wounds and ailments, pulled splinters, cleaned cuts, checked fevers, and wrapped sprained ankles. I wiped more noses and calmed more nerves than I could count. Some of those soldiers came in tough, limping from drills or clutching their stomachs, but once they sat down, once the mask slipped, you saw the boy still hiding inside the uniform. I learned their aches and fears and understood the quiet power of healing, not just with medicine but with presence. The pharmacy was a different battlefield, one where steadiness and compassion could do more than strength.

I spent about a year there, learning the rhythm of the work. The slow mornings, the long afternoons, the steady hum of conversation, charts, supplies, and care. For once, I wasn't out in the cold. I was in a place where people looked to me for help, and I found pride in meeting their needs. I wasn't just another number in a line of soldiers. I was "Murray" at the pharmacy window, and that meant something.

The Army paid better than anything I could've dreamed of back home. I sent money to Mama like a good son should. I bought myself a real wristwatch that ticked with authority and didn't lose time when it rained. I bought a pair of black leather boots that didn't leak when I walked through puddles. For the first time, I felt not just like a man, but like a man who could afford to be one.

After about three years of service, with my time in the Aleutians counted toward overseas duty, I received my honorable discharge. I had come into the Army and a boy rose behind a plow, with cotton under my nails and doubt in my eyes. But I walked out of those gates a man who had crossed states, oceans, and battle lines, emotionally and literally. I had eaten in mess halls with men from New York, Alabama, California, and Carolina. I froze under foreign skies and sweated under marching packs. I had earned respect, not demanded it. And that made all the difference.

From Kansas to California, from Alaska to the icy thresholds of Russia, I had marched, crawled, labored, and endured. I had learned how to survive in a world that didn't always want me to. And I had made it.

The world was shifting, too. The Korean War still raged far across the Pacific. Back home, the country was stirring with early tremors of change, Rosa Parks hadn't yet refused her seat, but Thurgood Marshall was winning cases, and the language of equality was starting to form in pulpits and town halls across the South. Something was waking up. And I was ready.

Ready to walk back into Louisiana, not as a barefoot country boy scraping a living from the red dirt, but as a man who had stood in the cold wind and sterile clinics, carrying machine guns and medicine alike. A man with a story to tell, with purpose rising in his chest, and with a fire that no field, no uniform, no system could ever put out.

CALIFORNIA DREAMING,

CALIFORNIA TRUTH

By the time I stepped out of the Army in 1953, I wasn't the same barefoot boy who'd once plowed behind a mule or walked into that recruiting office in Texarkana with nothing but ambition and calloused hands. I had served. I had saluted. I survived. I had stood watch through freezing nights in the Aleutians and drilled in the shadow of war with men from every walk of life. The Army didn't just give me a uniform, it gave me a spine. And when they handed me that crisp, folded discharge paper, it felt like more than an ending. It was a certificate of transformation. I had left as a boy from Bienville Parish. I came back as a man, battle-tested, sharp-eyed, and finally able to breathe with my chest out.

The young girls I'd known were women now, some married, some with babies already in their arms. One in particular, an old flame from before I left, told me she had waited for me, said she'd kept her heart sealed like a letter with my name on it. But the other girls, the younger ones, told a different story. "She didn't wait too long," they said. "She had a baby not long after you shipped out." I didn't press it. I didn't ask questions. Truth has a way of rising to the surface without being called. That moment made something clear to me: home had changed. And maybe, just maybe, so did I.

My shoes fit better now. My shoulders sat higher. And for the first time in my life, I didn't flinch when a White man looked me in the eye. I didn't duck my head. I didn't stammer. I didn't wait for permission to matter. I had carried a rifle, taken orders, polished boots until they gleamed like mirrors, and endured long stretches of silence where dignity was all a Black man could hold onto. I had earned respect, not because someone gave it, but because I had taken it for myself, day by day, mile by mile, uniform by uniform. And I wasn't about to give it up just because I was back in Louisiana.

Still, coming home wasn't the same as I thought it would be.

The South hadn't changed. The fields still whispered of sweat and sorrow. The cotton still bloomed like ghosts on every roadside. And though I had changed, too many people still wanted to treat me like I hadn't. I was grateful to be home, but not enough to stay. Something was burning in me, something restless, like a fuse waiting to catch. I'd seen too much sky, too many new faces, too many hints of a life beyond the rows of cane and cotton. I couldn't go back to being just another field hand, just another colored boy with a "yes sir" in my mouth. I wanted more. I needed more.

So, I tried the next logical step. College.

That fall, I enrolled at Grambling State University. I had enough money from the G.I. Bill to get started, and education might be the path forward. But the truth is, I wasn't ready. My body had returned to civilian life, but my spirit was still marching. I couldn't sit still in a classroom long enough to pretend I belonged there. I was wired tight, still bracing for inspection, still hearing reveille in the back of my mind. Discipline had saved me in the Army. But on that campus, it felt like a trap. I was a grown man surrounded by boys who'd never seen past the county line, and I didn't feel like I fit.

That's when Junior White showed up again. My cousin. My comrade. My Guardian Angel. My Chariot.

What I hadn't shared before, but what weighed more heavily on me the longer I thought about it, was what happened to Junior while I was stationed in Alaska. My days were spent behind pharmacy counters, drilling in formation, bracing against subzero winds, and studying skies that never stopped snowing. It was cold, routine, and, for the most part, safe. But Junior? He was sent to Korea. While I was stockpiling penicillin, he was ducking bullets. While I was counting pills, he was counting the seconds between mortar blasts. He saw things I didn't, and I never asked him to explain. I didn't need to. You could see it in his eyes.

Somewhere over there, in the chaos and gunfire, Junior got married. The details were foggy, intentionally, I think. He didn't offer much, and I didn't press. There are some stories a man keeps sealed to protect himself or the people he still wants to love. All I knew was that it didn't wrap up neatly when his tour ended. Junior didn't get an honorable discharge. He went AWOL, absent without leave, and came home carrying more than just a duffel bag. Maybe it was his wife's doing. Perhaps it wasn't. I didn't ask. I figured if he wanted to tell me, he would. And if he didn't, well, that was his right.

So, when he showed up back in Louisiana, thin, sharp, quiet, I didn't question the path he'd taken. I just saw my cousin, my brother in arms, the same man who had stood beside me in the recruiting line years before. He was back. And with him came a spark, a vision, a way out.

"Let's go west," he said. And just like that, the past didn't matter. I didn't care about the discharge papers or what had gone wrong. I was ready for California. So, I didn't hesitate. I packed up everything I had, my duffel bag, my discharge, and my grit, and followed my cousin westward toward the horizon. I wasn't running from Louisiana. I was chasing something bigger. Something freer. Something golden. I was chasing California.

California. Even the word felt like a dream. It was the land of sunshine and movie stars, orange groves, and wide highways. It was everything Louisiana wasn't, open, modern, fast-moving, full of motion and ambition. Back home, things stayed still for too long. The South was heavy with history, soaked in segregation. But California? That was the future. And I was hungry for it.

The bus ride was long, winding through deserts and hills, towns and cities I had never heard of. I remember watching the landscape change, how the red dirt gave way to golden fields, how the pine trees thinned, and how the skies seemed wider. I arrived with little money and had no job lined up, but I had a heart full of hope and was trained to work.

Junior White and I took odd jobs, lived modestly when we first arrived, and sent money back home when we could. We lived in neighborhoods full of Black folks who, like us, had come from Louisiana, Mississippi, and Texas, carrying stories, recipes, scars, and songs. There was a spirit of survival and ambition there, men working in shipyards, women cleaning homes, and children dreaming of college and California dreams.

We hit Los Angeles like a pair of wild cards. There were no plans, just grit. We found quick work hauling scrap metal, copper, brass, aluminum, from the junkyards around Alameda Street. It was hard, greasy, backbreaking work. We pulled rusted iron from heaps of wreckage, lifted tangled coils that cut your hands if you weren't careful, and tossed heavy pipes into battered trucks until our backs screamed.

But the pay was good, and on a good day, we could make $100 each, more money than we had ever seen picking cotton back home.

When I arrived in California, two of my first cousins, Earl Hall and John L. Daniels, had also recently completed their Army service. John L., ever the charismatic leader, quickly became the ringleader of our tight-knit group. We were players through and through. I stayed with my brother, Bates Murray, in a modest three-bedroom house in 2037 92nd Street in Watts. The size didn't matter; it could have been a single room, and we wouldn't have cared. Often, I'd return home to find the place filled with so many women that it was hard to get through the door.

It was a time of youthful exuberance and newfound freedom, a stark contrast to the disciplined life we'd left behind in the Army.

And we lived like it. We spent money just as fast as we made it. We bought wide-brimmed hats, crisp slacks, and cologne that made us smell like the downtown night. We filled our bellies with steak and biscuits and wiped our mouths with laughter. We cruised the city in borrowed cars with radios turned high, feeling like kings in chrome chariots. We called it "running the streets." Every Friday night was an adventure, packed dance halls, nightclubs thick with beer and smoke, jukeboxes wailing blues, and early rock 'n' roll. I crossed paths with more women than I could name, some danced close, some laughed loudly, and some were gone before I even asked their names. If I did ask their names, it would always be a blur, like verses in a song you feel more than you remember. But I remember the feeling, hot, fast, untouchable.

But California dreams are tricky things. They shine until they burn. One afternoon, we were riding through Hollywood. The palm trees leaned tall against the sky, and the storefronts gleamed. Junior handed me the keys to the old scrap truck. It was a beast of rust and noise, and I didn't know it had no brakes. We hit a hill. I tapped the brakes. Nothing. I pressed harder, but still nothing. I clipped one car, bounced into another, and sent a third spinning toward the sidewalk.

When the dust settled, I still gripped the wheel, my hands shaking like they belonged to someone else. Sirens echoed in the distance, and I knew then, California had taught me what Louisiana never could: even when you're moving fast, you can't outrun who you are or where you're from.

I stood before a California judge, license-less, registration-less, nearly senseless with fear. I expected jail. But the judge must've seen something in me. He fined me seven dollars and told me to get a license. I did. But when I returned to court, he revoked my new license. Lesson delivered. Message received.

That moment was my wake-up call. I wasn't built for that life, not the fast money or constant chase. California had its charms, but it didn't have roots. And I needed roots. I had come chasing gold but found the truth instead. And that truth was waiting back home.

I packed my bags quietly. I didn't need to talk about it. I just hummed the song my elders used to sing when they were ready to go home: "I'm going home tomorrow." And I did. Junior helped me pack. We rolled east in silence, leaving behind the neon glow, the nightclub smoke, the hustle. We traded it for red clay, front porches, and slow mornings that asked you to stay awhile. I didn't feel like I had failed. I felt like I had finally understood. My future wasn't out in the glitter, it was back in the ground that raised me. Back to Louisiana. Back to purpose. Back to the dreams that weren't loud or fast, but would last.

BACK TO GRAMBLING:

BUILDING A FUTURE

When I came home from California in the late fall of 1954, it felt like the dust of the West Coast was still clinging to my clothes, but my spirit had shifted. The glamor of the fast life, the quick cash, and the slick streets had lost their shine. I had gone to California chasing something, freedom, maybe, or escape, but what I found was that the real gold was back home, buried not in a city skyline but in the soil of my roots. I was ready to rebuild, to lay a foundation I could stand on for the rest of my life.

In January 1955, I enrolled at Grambling College under the Accelerated Plan, a tough, no-nonsense program created especially for veterans like me who weren't interested in wasting time. There would be no long summer breaks, no easing into the workload. We pushed through straight: spring, summer, fall, and winter. We didn't have time for leisure, our urgency came from service, from sacrifice, and from survival.

Grambling's campus wasn't glamorous. The old wooden dorms leaned like they had carried generations of hope on their backs. The cafeteria line stretched with anticipation, more than just for food, but for a future. The school buzzed with ambition. Young Black men and women filled every corner of that campus with dreams their parents and grandparents were never allowed to hold.

Even the football field hummed with purpose. Coach Eddie Robinson was already becoming a legend. He turned country boys into champions, many of whom would go on to the NFL. But it wasn't just about football, it was about proving that a small Black college in rural Louisiana could raise greatness. It felt like I was part of something beginning to roar.

The classrooms were charged with expectations. Our professors didn't coddle us. They challenged us. They knew the world outside those walls would not bend to us easily. We were sharpened with purpose. One professor in particular, Dr. Lewis Charles Goodwin, stood out. He headed the Social Studies department, and under his guidance, I soaked in knowledge like dry ground drinks in the rain. Government. History. Sociology. I wanted to understand how people and systems worked, and more importantly, I wanted to teach that truth with clarity and conviction. That's why I majored in social studies, with minors in speech and English, tools I would later use in classrooms, pulpits, and boardrooms of resistance.

Economics nearly knocked me out. The terms, "Gross National Product," "Federal Reserve," and "Chase Manhattan Bank", sounded like code from another world. To a boy raised on sharecropping and segregation, these concepts felt foreign. But I kept fighting. I had already crossed too many lines to turn back now.

Dorm life at Grambling was simple, strict, and tightly packed. Two of us were squeezed into each room, narrow bunks, a scratched-up pine dresser, a dented desk barely big enough for our books, and windows that creaked in the wind. The old dorm buildings leaned like they'd seen decades of boys come and go, each one chasing a dream too long denied. The scent of pine cleaner and old paper filled the halls. It wasn't luxurious, but it was sacred, it was ours.

A dorm dean lived among us to not just keep order but to model what it meant to walk with integrity and discipline. He didn't tolerate foolishness. Lights out meant lights out. There were curfews, inspections, and expectations. That kind of structure didn't bother me. The Army had already broken me in, and Grambling was just a new kind of formation, marching toward education instead of war.

Sunday was church day, with no exceptions. Every student had to attend one of the three local churches: Baptist, Methodist, or Catholic. We opted for the Catholic service most weekends, not out of devotion, but out of strategy. It ended earlier than the others, which meant we were first in line for Sunday dinner. And let me tell you, that plate, fried chicken, black-eyed peas, greens, and cornbread hot out of the pan, felt like communion. It was a small, unspoken tradition that turned the church into something more than spiritual, it became survival with a side of sweet tea.

The fluorescent lights buzzed low above our heads at night as we bent over textbooks and scribbled out assignments. The hallways held the smell of ambition, fried food from the cafeteria, old paperbacks passed down from one student to the next, sweat from boys who were grinding toward better futures. We were far from home, but we had each other. Some men cracked jokes until curfew. Others shared poetry, prayers, or plans for how they'd change their communities once they got out of school.

To make a little cash, I picked up some clippers and started cutting hair right there in the dorm. I wasn't a trained barber, but I could shape a clean hairline, keep the clippers oiled, and talk just enough trash to make my customers feel fresh. I would charge a dollar a head. It wasn't much, but it bought socks, snacks, notebooks, and dignity. That little hustle gave me the kind of pride no job title ever could.

If we had a few coins left on the weekend, we'd sneak off to Monroe or Ruston. Maybe catch a movie, shoot some pool, or dip into a juke joint where the jukebox played Fats Domino, and the girls laughed with their whole bodies. We didn't have much, but life was complete, and laughter came easy when the week was behind you and the world was still wide open. And even as we labored through our assignments, the world around us was catching fire. In 1954, the Supreme Court ruled in *Brown v. Board of Education* that school segregation was unconstitutional. It was a thunderclap, something we'd prayed for but never expected so soon. Then came 1955. The year Emmett Till, just fourteen years old, was lynched in Mississippi. His mother, brave beyond measure, laid his mutilated body in an open casket for the world to witness what hate could do. That same year, Rosa Parks refused to give up her seat on a Montgomery bus, and Dr. Martin Luther King Jr., barely known outside his church, stepped into the fight.

At Grambling, we felt those tremors. We talked about them in our dorms, in the cafeteria, and on walks between classes. The newspaper headlines might've been far away, but the pain and fire of those stories lived inside us. We knew the degrees we were earning weren't just tickets to better jobs. They were weapons. They were armor. They were tools for the fight unfolding in courtrooms, classrooms, and city streets. We weren't just students, we were soldiers in a quiet revolution, learning the language of freedom, one textbook at a time.

And somewhere between lectures, haircuts, and cafeteria lines, I met Mary Alice Kent. She was a home economics major, quiet in voice but strong in presence, the kind of young woman who didn't need to raise her voice to be noticed. She carried herself with poise, graceful, focused, and already moving like a woman who knew where she was headed. I was drawn to her instantly. Maybe it was how she plated her food, as if it were art, or perhaps it was how she spoke with purpose like every word had weight.

She would sometimes call me over after her lab and hand me a plate, fried chicken, collard greens, and hot rolls she had baked herself. It wasn't just a meal. It was care. It was something soft and grounding in a world where I was constantly pushing forward. We spent evenings talking about where we came from, what we hoped to do with our degrees, and what kind of lives we might build beyond Grambling's gates.

She was from Homer, not too far away, and her family welcomed me warmly whenever I visited. During our student teaching assignments, I was placed in Minden and Ruston; she was stationed back home in Homer. Some weekends, I'd drive to sit on her porch, eat supper with her folks, and feel like the world had slowed down long enough for us to dream.

We weren't loud with our affection. There were no promises made in the clouds. But there was a tenderness there, a belief in each other's becoming. And in those quiet, borrowed hours, I found something rare: peace.

When we graduated in 1957, she took a job teaching in rural Arkansas. I stayed behind, trying to find my place. The distance stretched. The calls came less. The visits stopped. The last time I saw her was Christmas of that year. We said goodbye without saying it. And life, as it often does, carried us in different directions.

But I never forgot her. She was part of the soil I stood on. Part of the foundation I was laying. And in a time when everything felt urgent and uncertain, Mary Alice Kent gave me something steady, something kind, something good.

In May of 1957, I graduated from Grambling College with a Bachelor's Degree in Social Studies. There were no television cameras, marching bands, or national headlines: just worn shoes, firm handshakes, and broad smiles. I walked across that wooden stage with more than a diploma in my hand, I carried every ancestor who'd been denied an education, every child in my hometown who needed to see what was possible, and every dream I'd ever whispered when I didn't think anyone was listening.

I didn't know exactly where the road would lead next. But I knew with absolute certainty, I wasn't going back. I was moving forward. And God willing, I was going to make something of this life that so many had bled, fought, and prayed to give me.

AFTER THE MARCH:

FAMILY, FRACTURE, AND A FUNERAL

After graduating from Grambling in May of 1957, I wasn't ready to slow down. I had my degree in hand and the weight of my family's prayers behind me, and I knew that somewhere out there, my next step was waiting.

But I didn't rush off to a job or another city right away. I stayed around the Ringgold for a while, visiting with old friends and helping Mama and Papa tend to things around the house. It was a strange, in-between season: I had accomplished something real, something most folks in my shoes never dreamed of. And yet, there was still restlessness in me. A sense that something was shifting in the air, not just in my own life but in our family. And then it happened.

In May of 1958, we buried Aunt Ophelia. She was one of Mama's sisters, wise, quiet, the kind of woman who didn't say much but made every word count. When she passed, it was like a soft pillar had fallen. Not loud. Not grand. But steady. All of Papa's children attended her funeral, a rare thing. Maybe the last time that all of them were in the same city. After that, we'd only gather in pieces.

Liberty Hill was full that weekend, full of cars, cousins, casseroles, and quiet tension. Folks came in from Shreveport, Houston, California. Some hadn't been home in years. Some came because they loved Ophelia. Others came because you're supposed to. But love and obligation sit heavy on the same porch, and the weight showed.

That day wasn't just a funeral, it was a reckoning.

People were in their best Sunday black, fans waving slowly under the sun. The service was beautiful, filled with hymns and whispered amens, but the moment we said the final "Ashes to ashes," it all started to turn. At the house, the heat thickened. Tempers rose. And when we walked into the kitchen for the repast, you could feel it: something was about to break.

Aunt Doris had offered to host dinner. She had the biggest house at the time, even if it didn't have air conditioning, and her pride was riding high. The living room was wall-to-wall people, sweat on brows, babies crying, dresses sticking to backs, fans going full speed and not helping a bit. Then came the turkey.

Aunt Mae, not Doris, stepped up to carve it. Just took the knife and started cutting, cool, clean strokes like it was hers to do. She had always been a take-charge kind of woman. Elegant, sharp-tongued when provoked. But that one motion, her hand slicing into the bird, was like a match to dry grass. Aunt Doris stood there frozen. Hurt and heat pooled in her eyes. She had cooked, hosted, set the table, and then Mae had taken the stage. No announcement. No ask. Whispers started. Then murmurs. Then, there were side-eyes and sharp little comments that only the family knew how to make. The kind that looks like smiles but cuts like blades.

Someone accused someone else of "always thinking they're better than everybody." Another cousin whispered that someone "ain't been home in years but think they run things." Tension poured into that hot kitchen like steam from a boiling pot. I heard someone mutter that Mae had "hidden meat in the back bedroom" to save it for her favorite folks. And whether it was true or not it didn't matter, it felt true in the moment, and that's all it took.

Some folks left before dessert. Some slammed doors. Others sat in the car with the engine running, cooling off more than just their bodies. You could feel relationships unraveling over turkey and sweet tea. And when the last plate was scraped, the last car backed out of that red clay driveway, we knew it was over.

That was the last time Papa's children came home together. After Ophelia died and that turkey got carved, we never gathered like that again. Funerals happened, sure. Weddings, births, more passings. But never again with that same full circle. Something had splintered.

Looking back, I realize we weren't just burying Ophelia, we were burying the last of a certain kind of unity. One shaped by front porch prayers, homemade biscuits, and Sunday school songs. After that day, the glue that held us together began to dry and crack. Some of us patched it up in later years. Others never quite did. And I don't know if pride or pain kept us apart. Maybe both.

So, I followed a familiar urge and headed north to Chicago, where the streets promised opportunity, and the skyline whispered ambition. This wasn't my first brush with the Windy City, but now, fresh from college, I thought maybe I could finally plant something there that would grow.

I made the trip with Horace Daniels, Sang, we called him, my cousin and Uncle Luke's son. Sang had a way about him; he was cool but grounded, always watching and always listening. He had been to Chicago before and knew the rhythm of the place, the pulse of it. I leaned on that. We were young Black men chasing possibility, walking streets paved with more than concrete, streets layered with risk, promise, and the unknown.

We stayed with my older brother, Lee Arthur Murray, and his wife, Pinky, in a modest apartment near the South Side, not far from Bronzeville. We were grateful for a warm bed, hot meals, and the quiet kind of brotherly understanding that didn't require a lot of words. By that time, Lee had built a life for himself in Chicago. He had opened his own barbershop, not just a chair in someone's kitchen, but a proper storefront with a sign in the window and regular clients from all walks of life. He had also started a family. Watching him juggle business, family, and dignity in a big city made a lasting impression. He wasn't just surviving, he was thriving. And though we never said it aloud, I admired him for that.

His barbershop was more than a place for haircuts. It was a hub. I'd sit in the corner sometimes, just listening to the men talk, about work, about women, about race, about whether the Sox had a chance that year. Between the buzzing clippers and the laughter, I could feel the city's pulse. But I also felt the tension: the sharpness beneath the surface, the quiet suspicion in a room when a White customer walked in. It was life in the North, freer, but not free.

Sang and I worked odd jobs, mostly construction, hauling lumber, laying concrete, and swinging sledgehammers from sunrise to quitting time. I remember one frigid morning, the wind coming off Lake Michigan cut through every layer of clothing I had. Sang and I were carrying cinder blocks across a job site, slipping on frozen mud, our fingers numb and raw. A White foreman barked at us to move faster. I looked at Sang and said, "Brother, I thought we left this behind in the South." He just grinned, teeth chattering, and said, "Same dirt, different accent."

I applied for a Civil Service job. I even tried my luck at the post office, thinking a federal gig might offer security. But every door felt heavier than expected, and every waiting room was a cold reminder that I was just another Southern boy with big dreams and no proper winter coat. The city didn't welcome me the way I had hoped.

In the late 1950s, Chicago was alive but also tense. Black families from the South were pouring in, chasing the same dream I was chasing: a fair wage, a real roof, a life without the daily humiliation of Jim Crow. The city was changing. Steel plants, meatpacking houses, and railyards had fed Black families for years, but those jobs were slipping away, and housing was tight. White flight was draining neighborhoods, and redlining made sure we stayed boxed in. Discrimination hadn't vanished, it had just traded hoods for policies.

I kept trying. But the wind in Chicago cut through you like a straight razor. It felt like the air itself was asking what you were made of. The sidewalks moved too fast. The people spoke like they didn't have time to care. Every time I stepped outside, the city reminded me: You don't belong here.

And maybe I didn't. I had come so far, from Ringgold to Fort Riley, from the Aleutians to Grambling, and now I was still searching for a place to plant my flag. But Chicago wasn't it. I crossed oceans and outlasted systems. Now, it was time to cross into purpose.

Then, one day, the phone rang. On the other end were two familiar voices, Spragley Marston and Benny Bennett, friends from back home. "Roy," they said, "we've got a job for you, teaching in Red River Parish. They need someone who knows how to lead a classroom." That was all I needed.

I packed my bags, this time with certainty, not searching, and boarded a bus heading south. The cold wind of Chicago was behind me. The warmth of Louisiana was ahead. I wasn't just going home, I was stepping into my calling.

Soon after, I arrived at Grand Bayou, a small rural Black school near where I had once picked cotton under that same Louisiana sun. I was stepping into my assignment.

The classroom became my battlefield, my pulpit, and my platform. I didn't show up to pass the time. I showed up to shape minds, challenge lies and teach the truth. That job wasn't just a paycheck, it was the beginning of everything.

A NEW LIFE BEGINS:

TEACHING, TRIALS, AND TENACITY

When I stepped through the doors of Grand Bayou School in August of 1958, I knew I wasn't just entering a job, I was stepping into my calling. The building itself was nothing fancy. Just a single-story wooden structure out in the countryside, with creaking floors, peeling paint, a sagging tin roof, and a potbelly stove that barely held off the chill of a Louisiana winter. But to me, it may as well have been a palace. For the first time, someone put "Mister" in front of my name; I was now called "Mr. Murray."

I was assigned to teach seventh and eighth-grade social studies, but the job didn't end there. In a school like Grand Bayou, if you were breathing, you were needed. I coached boys' basketball, drove the activity bus, ran morning devotionals, and on days the janitor didn't show, I grabbed a mop and cleaned the floors. There was no such thing as "not my job." We were there for the children, and they were watching everything.

The classrooms had textbooks with missing pages, "DISCARD" stamped on the covers, hand-me-downs from the White schools. The desks wobbled. The chalkboards were faded. But those kids? They were bright. They were hungry. Not just for food, though some came to school with nothing more than a biscuit or syrup sandwich in a brown bag, but for knowledge. They wanted to learn. They wanted to rise. And I had come to teach them how.

I stood before them every morning holding a chalk stick like a sword. I didn't just teach about government or geography, I taught how to stand tall in a world that often told you to stay small. I taught them how laws worked, how history was made, and how language could be used as a shield and a weapon. We read aloud. We debated. We wrote essays with shaky grammar but powerful truth.

I made lesson plans by hand, one for each subject. Five days a week, two subjects, one teacher. I kept a copy in the principal's office in case I was ever out, and a substitute had to step in. But most days, I was there. Rain or shine, broken radiator or not, I showed up. Because these children deserved consistency in a world that too often gave them chaos.

And when the bell rang at the end of the day, the work didn't stop. Some students stayed behind for tutoring. Others just wanted to talk. Some wanted someone to listen. And I was there for that, too. I had been where they were. I had walked to school in worn shoes, studied by a kerosene lamp, and wondered if I mattered. Now it was my turn to make sure they knew that they did.

That first year at Grand Bayou shaped everything that came after. It was there that I learned that teaching wasn't just about curriculum, it was about calling. It was about pouring yourself into someone else, trusting that one day, they'd rise and carry it forward.

And it was there, in that quiet country school, where I first began to see the path I would walk for the rest of my life, not just as a teacher, but as a builder of people.

FROM RESTLESS TO ROOTED: LOVE, LAND, AND LEGACY

Before I met Sarah, I wasn't thinking about settling down. I dated freely, many women, if I'm honest. Not carelessly, but without deep intention. I enjoyed the company, the conversation, and the companionship. I wasn't looking forever. At that point in my life, I was still running. Still discovering who I was.

There was a young woman I saw from time to time, a Fritz girl. It wasn't serious. No commitment, just occasional company. So, when I later heard she was pregnant and claiming the child was mine, I didn't believe it. Not then. We hadn't been in a real relationship, and I had no way to know for sure.

It was around that same time that I met Sarah Reliford.

We met at a church picnic in Ringgold, beneath the slanting shade of a wide oak tree. The air was thick with barbecue smoke, gospel music, and the laughter of barefoot children darting across the grass. The older men sat under canvas tarps, playing checkers and trading slow, steady conversations like verses from a hymn. And there, just off to the side, stood Sarah, in a butter-yellow dress, the sunlight catching her like a blessing. She wasn't loud or showy. She didn't have to be. When she smiled, the world seemed to pause.

We started talking about school, family, and dreams we hadn't dared speak aloud before. She was thoughtful and soft-spoken, but strong in a way that didn't need to announce itself. I could tell her people had raised her with love and faith, and a quiet confidence that didn't hinge on anyone else's opinion. With respect, patience, and purpose, I courted her the right way. We went to church together, shared porch swings after supper, and began to stitch our lives together, piece by piece. Around Sarah, I didn't have to perform. She never asked for more than the truth. And I gave it.

Then, just as we were preparing for marriage, I got word that the Fritz girl had given birth to a baby boy. She named him Ricky Roy Murray.

I still wasn't convinced he was mine. I had no proof. But I couldn't shake its weight. I kept it to myself at the time. I was already walking a different path guided by something more profound.

And maybe that moment was God's way of nudging me, reminding me that life was serious, and real love shouldn't be delayed. So, I made a decision.

I picked up the phone and called Spragley Marston, a man I trusted. I asked him to go to Grambling and bring Sarah home. He did. That Friday, she came back. And on Sunday, September 28, 1958, Sarah and I were married on the front porch of her parents' home in Ringgold, Louisiana. Her father was away, working near the Sunshine Bridge in South Louisiana. Her mother had accompanied her husband in South Louisiana. Still, her sisters stood proudly beside us,

Rovella, her oldest sister, Revelma, older sister, Revelma's husband William "Buddy" Thomas, and others gathered under a warm afternoon sky. Reverend Moore performed the ceremony, holding a weathered Bible in one hand and our future in the other. The sun was warm, the cicadas were singing, and the sky was clear enough to make you believe in things you hadn't seen yet.

Just before the wedding, I bought a 1958 Ford and accepted my first teaching job with the Red River Parish School Board. I now had a wife, a career with purpose, and a steady hand on the wheel. As one of my old high school teachers said when he passed by and saw me, "A new car, a new wife, and a new job." And he was right. All of it was new, and it felt right.

After the wedding, Sarah and I moved into my grandfather's old house, sharing space with my mother, Lucille, and Papa Alfred Daniels. It wasn't fancy. The floors sagged, the woodstove smoked, and the summers were cooled only by open windows and hand fans. But it was home. We saved every penny we could, dreaming of our own house one day. We didn't have much, but we had enough. And more importantly, we had each other. One step at a time. One prayer at a time. One brick at a time.

Looking back, I know now that all those restless days of searching, running, and stumbling led me here, to this woman, this life, this foundation. And I thank God I had the sense to stop and recognize it.

We married when Black America was beginning to stand taller than ever before. In 1957, the Civil Rights Act, the first since Reconstruction, had been passed. Sit-ins were starting to spread, and Dr. King was gaining national recognition. In our small way, Sarah and I were part of that rising tide. Our marriage, our education, our determination, all acts of quiet resistance against a world that had told us to stay small.

It wasn't just a commitment. It was a declaration. We had come too far, survived too much, and dreamed too big to ever turn back now.

RAISING A FAMILY AND TEACHING

THROUGH THE 60s

The 1960s rolled in like a storm, heavy with change, hope, and danger. Right there in the thick of it, building a life, raising a family, and teaching young Black minds, stood me, determined to forge a better future with every step.

We didn't just build a house, we built a beginning out of raw timber, scraped knuckles, and prayers whispered between hammer swings. The address was Route 1 Box 58, a modest stretch of land tucked into the clay-rich soil of Red River and Bienville Parishes, and every nail we drove into those boards was a declaration: We belong here. We are building something no one can take away.

After school let out, I'd shed my tie and classroom voice, grab my work boots, and head straight to the lot. The ground was uneven, the sun unforgiving, and the tools were often borrowed. But I showed up every evening with a hammer in one hand and hope in the other. Ed Moore, a master with a saw and a quiet spirit, was the lead carpenter. But he wasn't alone. William Hayden and John Loveless came nearly every day after work, their shirts soaked with the honest sweat of neighbors who knew that community wasn't something you talked about, it was something you built.

We had no blueprints, just rough sketches on notebook paper. No bank loans, just folded-up bills from church members and jars of saved change. No heavy machinery, just calloused hands and faith that wouldn't bend. We didn't pour concrete with a crew, we mixed it ourselves, one wheelbarrow at a time. The framing rose slowly, the planks nailed with rhythm and resolve. The smell of sawdust clung to our skin. The sound of hammers echoed into the trees like gospel.

By the time Kendell was born in February 1960, the house was barely more than a frame with four walls, no running water, and a roof that still leaked when it rained. But it was standing. And it was ours. We brought our baby boy home into a world still under construction, wrapped not just in blankets but in the unspoken vows of every man who had laid hands on that home: *this child would have more than we did.*

The bathroom was unfinished, just pipes and wood and a prayer. We heated water on the stove and bathed the baby in a basin. The nights were cold; the wind pushed through every crack in the walls. Sarah nursed Kendell while I sat nearby, sketching out the next day's lesson plans, and the next layer of insulation I'd need to keep this fragile dream from freezing over. The butane heater hummed in the background, a quiet reminder that we were making do, building something solid out of something barely standing.

That house became more than shelter. Standing on the side of that highway with no frills and no apologies, it became a symbol. It was a story nailed into wood grain, of a teacher, a wife, a baby, and a community bold enough to believe that Black folks could build not just survival but stability.

We built with calloused hands, aching backs, empty pockets, and full hearts. We built with scripture in our bones and sawdust in our lungs. And when we lay down to sleep, on mattresses set atop plywood floors, we didn't dream of more. We were already living the dream.

Two years after Kendell was born, on July 4, 1962, Sarah gave birth to our second child, a daughter we named Jacqueline Kennedy Murray. We named her after the First Lady of the United States, Jacqueline Kennedy, who carried herself with a kind of grace, quiet strength, and elegance that Black women like Sarah had long modeled, even if the world didn't give them the same applause. That year, the country was caught between hope and heartbreak, but in our little corner of Louisiana, under a sky ablaze with fireworks, a firecracker child was born on Independence Day.

Jackie's birth came right in the middle of building our home, and I remember coming from school, picking up my hammer, and finishing a few boards before heading to the hospital. We didn't have much, but we had what mattered. And when Sarah came home with that baby girl in her arms, the house was unfinished but ready. There was no running water, no working bathroom, but there was warmth, family, and the laughter of a growing future. That house stood as both a shelter and a promise.

In February 1964, Roy Daniel Jr. was born. That boy came into the world full of spirit, with his mama's sweetheart and my stubborn streak. We could already tell he would speak his mind before he could spell it. By the time Roy Jr. arrived, the house was starting to feel full, but we didn't mind. We just made room, with extra hands, extra faith, and extra prayers.

Then, in 1967, Patrick Henry arrived. By that time, I was teaching a unit on the American Revolution. We were covering the speeches of men like Patrick Henry, who declared, "Give me liberty or give me death." The words stuck with me. I thought about the kind of country I was trying to raise my children in. About the freedom I wanted for them, not just from laws but from fear, ignorance, and limitation. So we gave our last baby a name full of fight. He was the exclamation point at the end of a chapter that had started with uncertainty but had been written in love.

Four children in seven years. That house on Highway 4 was noisy, bottles rattling on the counter, Sunday shoes lined up by the door, church dresses hanging to dry, homework spread across the table. There were nights when I graded papers by a dim table lamp while one child cried, another spilled juice, and Sarah tried to coax dinner onto plates that sometimes didn't hold much. But those were good years, the kind of years that build a man's soul, brick by brick.

Money was tight. Tempers got short. But the love we poured into that home was richer than any paycheck. And through it all, Sarah kept her calm. She wasn't just raising children, she was building character, shaping hearts, and holding our house together with faith, flour, and fortitude.

As I rocked babies and read textbooks by lamplight, I knew I wasn't just teaching in the classroom, I was teaching at home, preparing the next generation to walk taller, speak louder, and expect more.

In the middle of those hectic years, raising four children, building a house by hand, and teaching full-time, I never stopped learning. I enrolled in a graduate program through Louisiana State University, taking night classes in Shreveport while balancing the demands of my classroom and young family. During the summers of 1966 and 1967, I traveled down to Baton Rouge, studying in classrooms with other working teachers, all of us chasing a better future for ourselves and our students. In 1967, I earned my Master's Degree in Administration and Supervision, a rare achievement for a Black teacher in Red River Parish at the time. Later, I would go on to earn my Plus-30 credential from Northeastern, qualifying me for the highest pay scale the school system offered. I didn't just want a raise, I wanted the tools to lead, guide, and stand firm when the system tried to fold us in. Those degrees weren't just for me. They were for every child who'd ever been told there weren't enough.

As my family grew, so did my responsibilities in the classroom. I remained at Grand Bayou School, an all-Black country school nestled down a dusty road, for twelve whole years. Integration wouldn't arrive until 1970, so throughout the 1960s, my mission was clear: educate, empower, and equip Black children with the knowledge and confidence the world too often tried to deny them.

The building hadn't changed, not really. It was still the same single-story wooden frame with peeling paint and creaking floors, standing like it always had against the backdrop of pine and red clay. The desks were still scared with names, and the windows still rattled when the wind picked up. The books were still stamped "DISCARD" in faded ink, their pages torn, their spines cracked, their stories incomplete. But something else was different, we were gaining momentum.

You could feel it in the way students sat up straighter, how they clutched their notebooks with purpose. Their lunch pails still held biscuits with syrup, or a strip of fatback wrapped in wax paper, but their minds were stretching beyond those walls. We might not have had new books, but we had a new fire. And that, sometimes, was more than enough.

I was still teaching social studies, civics, government, and Louisiana history, but by then, the way I taught them had deepened. The textbooks hadn't changed, they still skipped over our stories, still sanitized our struggle, but I didn't let that stop me. Just like before, I wove Black history into every lesson, threading truth through the gaps the books refused to fill. I taught them about Booker T. Washington at Tuskegee, Marcus Garvey's Black Star Line, and Harriet Tubman, who didn't come here to be a slave and sure didn't die one. I reminded them that the first Africans landed in Virginia in 1619, before the Pilgrims ever set foot on Plymouth Rock, and that our history didn't begin in chains, and it wouldn't end in silence. The message hadn't changed, but the moment had. The world outside was stirring, and inside that classroom, we were preparing to meet it.

My classroom was still my battlefield, and the chalk in my hand was still my sword, but by now, I wielded it with more precision, more purpose. I had seen what education could do, and I refused to lower the bar. I didn't demand perfection, I demanded presence, effort, and engagement. My students still wrote speeches, debated real-world issues, and learned to speak their truths with clarity and conviction. I assigned *If* by Rudyard Kipling, speeches by Dr. King, and passages from our own hidden heroes, words that helped them stand taller than their circumstances. And in time, some of those students did just that. They became principals, preachers, business owners, and even mayors. Years later, many came back to tell me it all started in that classroom, with a question

I made them answer out loud or a truth I refused to let them ignore.

I wasn't just a teacher, I was still a coach, too. I took boys with hand-me-down sneakers, raw talent, and restless energy and shaped them into a team. I hadn't studied coaching at Grambling, but experience has a way of training you fast. I taught them how to move with discipline, how to run plays with purpose, and how to carry themselves like they belonged, on the court and in the world. We rode in beat-up buses down dirt roads to tiny schoolyards and country churches, singing spirituals to calm our nerves and eating peanut butter sandwiches packed in brown paper bags. We didn't always win on the scoreboard, but we played with heart. And the folks in our community, mamas, deacons, grandmothers, packed those gym bleachers like we were championship-bound.

And I drove that old activity bus myself, no assistant, no fanfare. Just a whistle, a clipboard, and a head full of hope.

I'd come home late, rock babies to sleep with one arm, help Sarah get supper on the table with the other, and then sit by the soft glow of a desk lamp grading essays into the night. It was a grind, but it was also a calling. And even in my exhaustion, I knew I was doing holy work.

That stretch of years before integration wasn't easy, but it was holy work. It was the slow, steady shaping of minds and spirits. It was proof that even in the margins, even in forgotten schoolhouses with broken windows and borrowed supplies, Black excellence could rise, and did, day after day, under the sound of my voice and the scratch of pencils on paper.

Meanwhile, the world beyond Ringgold was catching fire. In 1960, the Greensboro sit-ins made national headlines as four young Black college students refused to leave a Whites-only lunch counter, daring the system to confront their dignity. In 1961, the Freedom Riders boarded buses headed straight through the belly of the Deep South, rolling into flames, fists, and jail cells with nothing but conviction in their pockets. In 1963, Dr. Martin Luther King Jr. stood on the steps of the Lincoln Memorial and declared to the nation, "I have a dream," as more than 250,000 people listened with tears in their eyes and hope in their hearts.

I remember sitting in our living room that evening, the radio humming with the news, its tiny speaker delivering history to our ears. I held Sarah's hand in one of mine and rocked one of our babies with the other. The baby was dozing, and the house was quiet except for the broadcast. As King's voice rose and broke across the airwaves, I remember thinking: *Would that dream ever reach all the way down here to our dusty Louisiana backroads? To Grand Bayou? To Highway 4?*

That same year, in Birmingham, Alabama, the world watched in horror as fire hoses and police dogs were turned on children, Black schoolchildren marching for justice, their small frames thrown across sidewalks and churchyards like they were nothing. The images shocked the conscience of a nation, but to us in the South, it wasn't new. It was just finally being seen.

In 1964, the Civil Rights Act was signed into law. For the first time in American history, segregation in public places was outlawed, and employers could no longer legally discriminate based on race. On paper, we were equal. But in Louisiana, in the bayous, in the cotton fields, in the schoolrooms and storefronts, the old ways didn't vanish. They dug in deeper.

In 1965, the Red River Parish school board announced integration was coming. At first, it was voluntary. Only the bravest Black families dared to send their children to the White schools. It felt like sending them into battle without armor. Tensions rose like floodwater. There were whispers in barbershops, warnings at gas stations, and long stares from across grocery aisles. And then came the White flight, whole families pulling their children out of public schools and opening private "segregation academies" overnight.

We felt the ground shifting beneath our feet. Full-scale integration wouldn't come until 1970, but even in those mid-sixties' years, we knew change was barreling toward us whether we were ready or not. For now, I stayed at Grand Bayou, teaching my students, and my own children at home, that they were just as worthy, just as brilliant, and just as strong as anyone else walking this earth.

We were moving forward, but every step came with a cost.

When John F. Kennedy was assassinated in 1963, I was standing in my classroom at Grand Bayou. The news came like a slap, sharp and sudden. For the first time, many of us had felt like there was someone in the White House who at least *saw* us, who wanted to move the country forward, even if the system around him dragged its feet. When he died, it was like a door had slammed shut. The light dimmed. Hope didn't disappear, but it staggered.

Then came Malcolm. In 1965, they gunned him down in Harlem, right in front of his own people. He had been changing, evolving, and while his message was sharper than King's, it cut through a different kind of truth. He was teaching us to stand on our own, to build our own, to stop begging for seats at tables that had never welcomed us. When he was killed, it felt like we had lost not just a man but a compass.

And then, Dr. King. I met him once, briefly, in 1966 while visiting Chicago. He had just spoken at a church near Soldier Field. I shook his hand. He was smaller than I expected, soft-spoken in person, but he carried something you could feel, like he knew his time was short, but the work had to be done anyway. When they killed him in Memphis in 1968, I wept. I didn't cry loudly, I just sat on the edge of the bed, held Sarah's hand, and stared at the radio as the voice reported the impossible. He had been in town to support garbage workers. Garbage workers. A man who could've been anywhere, doing anything, chose to stand with the overlooked. And they shot him for it.

At that moment, everything felt fragile. We had lost our North Star. But even in my grief, I knew, they could kill the man, but they couldn't kill the message. We had to keep going. Keep marching. Keep teaching. Keep standing.

Even though they had just killed our leaders, the march would continue because our leaders had passed us the torch. And through all of it, through the marches, the court orders, the speeches, and the assassinations, one thing carried us: faith.

Every Sunday, we packed into Liberty Hill Church, shoulder to shoulder, on old wooden pews that creaked under the weight of generations. We sang with our whole hearts, "We Shall Overcome," "I'm So Glad Trouble Don't Last Always," and "I Don't Feel No Ways Tired." The choir didn't just lift melodies; they lifted burdens, lifted the week's exhaustion, lifted us. When the world felt too heavy, we leaned on each other and leaned on God. We knew this struggle was bigger than any one man or one moment, it would take all of us. Standing together and marching together and believing together.

But faith alone didn't build change, it had to be put to work. And in those turbulent years, I worked.

By the mid-1960s, I was no longer just a teacher. I had become a community leader, an organizer, and a voice for justice in a parish that wasn't used to hearing Black men speak with authority. I joined the NAACP and helped organize the local voter league, what others might have called the League of Women Voters, but in our corner of Louisiana, we simply called it "The Voter's League." I eventually became its president in Ringgold. Titles didn't matter as much as the mission: we were determined to get our people to the polls, no matter how many hurdles were thrown in our path.

Right alongside me was my uncle by marriage and my mentor by calling, Clearance D. Hall, known around town as C.D. Hall, but always "Uncle Clearance" to me. He was a tall, stout man with fair skin, a booming presence, and the kind of authority that made people straighten up when he entered a room. Married to my mother's sister, Aunt Doris, he was like a second father to me, a man who never hesitated to speak up, stand up, or show up. As president of the local NAACP, he was deeply respected, and together, we formed a powerful tag team in the fight for civil rights right here in Ringgold.

We were the ones folks called when the law came down wrong. If a boy was locked up unjustly or a protester jailed without cause, our phone would ring, it didn't matter if it was midnight or Sunday morning. Uncle Clearance and I would get in the car and go get them out. Not because we had money or clout but because we had conviction. We believed in the power of presence. And we knew that showing up, especially as Black men in the Deep South, was itself a revolutionary act.

We held meetings in schoolhouses, churches, and front porches, anywhere we could gather without interruption. We registered voters under dim overhead bulbs and trained neighbors on how to fill out ballots, how to speak their names boldly at courthouses, and how to stand tall in the face of intimidation. It wasn't just about the right to vote. It was about dignity, about walking into a polling place with your head high, knowing your voice mattered.

That movement wasn't just national, it was local. It was ours. And in Ringgold, we were carrying the torch.

In 1967, I was elected president of the Fourth District of the Louisiana Education Association, overseeing Red River, Bienville, and DeSoto Parishes. It wasn't just a title, it was a responsibility. I wrote weekly for the *Shreveport Sun*, penning columns that challenged the silence of injustice and encouraged Black teachers to raise their voices, not just their chalk.

When a Black man in Ringgold was killed after being accused of speaking to a White woman, our community didn't stay quiet. We formed a coalition and filed a civil suit, an act almost unheard of in a rural Louisiana town at that time. I wasn't in the courtroom, but I was in the pews and the planning meetings. I helped draft letters, make calls, and organize rides to hearings. We didn't win every fight, but we made them fight us. And in doing so, we made them see us. During those same years, I was also a proud and active member of the Prince Hall Masonic Lodge, a fraternal order that had long been a backbone of leadership and service in the Black community. The Lodge wasn't just ritual and regalia, it was brotherhood, discipline, and legacy. Through it, I was connected to a lineage of Black men who had led in times of peril and purpose, men who believed in truth, justice, charity, and the betterment of our people. The Lodge helped sharpen my leadership, grounded me in moral duty, and strengthened my voice when the fight demanded more than words.

Activism wasn't just about marches and speeches, it was about consistency. Showing up. Speaking truth. And keeping the pressure on until something cracked. Some folks thought we were pushing too hard. Others thought we weren't pushing hard enough. But we didn't stop. Couldn't stop. Because too many people had stopped before us, and we knew the cost of silence.

By the end of the 1960s, my life was complete. I had a strong marriage to Sarah, four children who were growing up fast, a steady job that allowed me to shape young minds, and a place in something larger than myself. I wasn't in the newspapers. I wasn't in Selma or Montgomery or D.C. I wasn't shouting through megaphones or dodging tear gas. But in my classroom, in my home, in my church, every single day, I fought. For truth. For dignity. For change.

Every night, after tucking in the kids and grading one last set of papers, I'd kneel beside our bed, tired in body but strong in spirit, and whisper the same prayer: "Lord, help me stand strong. For them. For the ones coming after me." The fight wasn't over yet. But we were closer than we had ever been. And so, I kept showing up. In classrooms and courtrooms, at church meetings and family dinners, in the quiet corners where change begins. The 1960s had tested us, but we held the line. We stood tall, even when the weight was heavy. And as a new decade dawned, I didn't yet know what the 1970s would bring. But I knew this much: I was ready. Rooted in faith, lifted by community, and surrounded by love, I stepped forward, still fighting, still teaching, still believing, because the work wasn't finished. Not by a long shot.

COMPLETE INTEGRATION AND

SURVIVING THE 70s

The 1960s brought change. But the 1970s? That was the storm. Not a quick thunderclap, but a slow, rolling storm that tested everything I believed in. It tested my calling, character, classroom, and community. It asked whether the work I had poured into my students for over a decade would be recognized in this new era of so-called progress, or whether everything we had built at Grand Bayou would be cast aside in the name of change.

After twelve years teaching at Grand Bayou, a proud little Black school tucked down a dusty road where I had taught generations of children, coached their teams, and even taught my own, I was reassigned to Coushatta High School in 1970. That year, the federal courts finally forced the Red River Parish School Board to implement full integration. Grand Bayou and the other small Black schools were closed, and Black and White students from every corner of the parish,

Martin, Hall Summit, Springville, and Hanna, were thrown together in unfamiliar classrooms. It was the first time we all sat side by side, Black and White students, Black and White teachers, all under the same roof. Legally, it was integration. Emotionally, it was something else entirely.

The moment I walked through the doors of Coushatta High, I could feel a tension thick in the air. Not loud. Not violent. But present, like a storm hovering above, waiting to break. Some White teachers gave me curt nods. Others looked past me like I wasn't there. Some White students folded their arms, staring at me with stone-cold silence. They weren't used to being taught by someone like me. And some Black students, confused by the sudden shift, sat quietly, unsure whether they still belonged.

For the first two weeks, I had no students and no classroom. Despite having a master's degree from LSU, one of the first held by a Black teacher in the parish, I was told nothing. No explanation. No apology. I reported to school each morning and was told to sit in the library. No desk. No duties. Just a chair. Just a paycheck. I didn't complain. I didn't make a fuss. I just waited. I had come too far, earned too much, and sacrificed too deeply to let that silence shake me.

When they finally called me in, they handed me a schedule: four hours of civics and one hour of tenth-grade English. That was fine by me. I had taught that same civics book for so long that I could recite it chapter by chapter. My students used to call me "Mr. Civics." I wore the name like a badge of honor.

And slowly, things began to shift. Some of the White students, particularly the girls, began to warm up. One day after class, a few of them asked if I wanted to learn how to play tennis. I'd never picked up a racket in my life, but I said yes. We went to the court, and they patiently and kindly taught me how to swing, serve, and play the game. We laughed. We learned from each other. It wasn't written in any court ruling or printed in any textbook, but that's when real integration started: in small, human moments where respect took root.

Still, not all challenges were so subtle. My principal, H. Truman Crawford, called me "Murray" whenever he addressed me, but insisted I call him "Mr. Crawford." One day, I asked him calmly why that was the case. He looked at me and said, "I want to feel close to you." I smiled politely. I didn't argue. I let his answer hang in the air. I had learned long ago that dignity is not something you demand with your voice, it's something you carry with your presence.

There was another day when he stormed into my classroom, angry about a civics test I had given. "You wrote that Black people arrived in America before the Pilgrims," he said, waving the paper in his hand like it was a crime. Without raising my voice, I walked to his bookshelf, pulled down a textbook, flipped to the timeline, and pointed: "1619, the first Africans arrive in Virginia. 1620, the Pilgrims land at

Plymouth Rock." He looked at the page, closed the book, and said nothing. That was the end of that.

In those early years of integration, I learned that you don't always have to shout. Sometimes, the truth speaks loud enough on its own.

Outside the classroom, I organized voter registration drives, wrote for the *Shreveport Sun*, and served as president of the Fourth District of the Louisiana Education Association. I spoke up when they wanted to silence us. I stood when others sat. And through it all, I kept praying: "Lord, help me stand strong for the ones coming after me."

But the storms of the 1970s weren't just political. They weren't just fought in the halls of schools or the streets of Selma. Some of the fiercest battles I faced came from within, from grief, responsibility, and reckoning with the ones who made me.

In 1973, I lost my grandfather, Papa Alfred Daniels, the quiet giant of our family, at the age of 104. He was more than the eighty-three acres that he owned. He was the anchor that kept generations steady, the voice that seldom spoke but always mattered. As the years crept in and his mind began to dim, I became his caregiver. My mother, by then, was elderly and could no longer carry the weight. I placed him in the elder care home in Coushatta, just a few miles from my job. I'd visit during the week, and every weekend, without fail, I'd bring him home.

He was still strong in his body, but confusion haunted his eyes. One day, I arrived and learned he had struck a nurse, not out of malice, but disorientation. He didn't know who she was. That moment crushed me. To see the man who had carried me as a child, now unrecognizable to himself, it broke something inside of me.

At the same time, Papa was beginning to slow down, his body still strong, but his mind wandering through a fog, I found myself drawn into another kind of heartbreak. Uncle Luke and Aunt Bob, both well up in age, had taken in their granddaughter, Denise Daniels. We called her Niecy. She was the daughter of Horace "Sang" Daniels, Uncle Luke's son, and a light in every room she entered. Smart, sharp, full of promise. Niecy wasn't just pretty, she glowed. The kind of beauty that whispered instead of shouted. She was quick with a joke, faster with a book, and carried herself with quiet confidence that made you look twice. She wasn't just a bright child. She was radiant. And then something changed. At first, it was subtle. She began forgetting things. Her words would slur for a moment, then catch themselves. She started to lose her balance. The sparkle in her eyes dimmed, not all at once, but like a candle fighting the wind. The doctors said it was a tumor. In her brain. Deep, dangerous, and growing. Those words hung in the air like smoke, choking, heavy, impossible to grasp.

Uncle Luke and Aunt Bob did what they could. But they were already weathered by time, worn thin from raising children and grandchildren alike. So I stepped in. Without fanfare, without discussion. I became Niecy's driver, escort, and prayer partner on wheels. I drove her to cancer treatments in Shreveport, sometimes as far as Dallas. Those trips felt like pilgrimages, long, quiet rides through pine-lined highways and broken two-lane roads. She would ride beside me, her head resting softly against the window, her breath shallow but steady. Sometimes we talked about God, about music, about her dreams. Other times, she would close her eyes, holding on, and I would pray under my breath with every passing mile. I didn't have the answers. But I had a car, a willing heart, and the desperate faith that maybe showing up counted for something. And it did.

Because out of that pain, out of Niecy's illness and Papa's failing health, something holy began to grow. What started as a small prayer gathering, just a handful of neighbors in someone's living room, kneeling by couches, whispering the names of the ones we loved, became a movement. We called it the *Wednesday Night Prayer Meeting*. At first, it was just us. Family. Friends. A few worn Bibles. A hymn was sung softly. But like all things rooted in love, it didn't stay small for long. Soon, the living rooms couldn't hold us.

We began moving from house to house, then from church to church. We didn't have a roster or a budget. What we had was belief, raw and ready. We had tambourines, testimonies, and voices cracked with sorrow but strong with praise. We gathered every Wednesday night, rain or shine, with our shoes off and hearts open, asking God to spare Niecy, to steady Papa, to hold back the tide of grief we saw coming. We prayed with urgency. With fire. With tears that soaked wood floors and carpet threads alike.

And then came Oretha Daniels, my neighbor and my cousin by marriage, the wife of Joe Louis Daniels, one of Uncle Luke's sons. Oretha had a voice that could hush a room and a spirit that moved like wind through dry grass, gentle but undeniable. She stepped into that growing circle of prayer and didn't just participate. She led. With grace. With power.

With faith that could tear down walls. She became the president of what we came to call the *Ringgold Prayer Band*, and under her leadership, what started as a whisper became a shout.

People came from all over, members of Baptist, CME, Pentecostal, and even Catholic churches, all under one banner: prayer. We sang, wept, laid hands, and anointed ourselves with oil. We believed. And if ever there was a miracle we hoped for, it was Niecy.

But not every miracle looks the way we want it to.

Niecy lost her battle. She slipped away slowly, softly, like a sigh carried off on the wind. One day, she was there, frail but smiling, and the next, she was gone. The house felt colder. The roads felt longer. And there was an empty seat beside me in the car that no one else could fill. We buried her with flowers and heartbreak, with scripture and songs that said, "He makes no mistakes," even though our hearts were breaking with questions.

Not long after, Papa followed, like two stars falling from the same sky, one after the other.

But here's the part that lives on: out of their sickness came the Prayer Band. Out of their suffering came unity. Out of their silence came a sound, of voices raised, of burdens lifted, of a community reminded that even in our sorrow, we are never alone.

When Papa passed, we laid him to rest after a service at Liberty Hill Church, surrounded by old songs and older sorrow. At the funeral, my mother, his eldest daughter, cried out from her soul, *"Papa, I'm coming to join you!"* Her voice cracked through the sanctuary like thunder. And I remembered what the scripture says: life and death are in the power of the tongue.

I had built my home on Papa's land, tucked into the same soil he had once walked with pride and purpose. And after he passed, I felt a responsibility deeper than inheritance, I felt legacy calling. I didn't want the land sold, cut up, or forgotten. I wanted to protect what he had worked for and preserve the ground that had anchored our family for generations. So, I began purchasing the heir property, parcel by parcel, handshake by handshake. Over time, I acquired fifty-three of his original eighty-three acres. Not for profit. Not for prestige. But to keep his name alive in the roots and rows, in the fields where he once stood tall. I didn't just own that land. I honored it.

Not long after that funeral, Mama's cry, *"Papa, I'm coming to join you!"*, began to take on the weight of prophecy. Grief hung on her like a heavy coat she couldn't shrug off. She started spending more time in San Diego, living with my sister Katherine, trying to find new air, new light, new hope. She needed rest, and Katherine did her best to give her comfort. But the body keeps score, and the heartbreak didn't just stay in her spirit, it pressed against her chest.

While out there on the West Coast, far from the red clay roads and pine trees of Ringgold, Mama suffered a massive heart attack. The kind that doesn't ask for permission. The kind that stops everything. When the call came, I dropped everything. I boarded a plane with my hands shaking prayers spilling out of my mouth like water. By the time I reached her side, she was lying in a hospital bed, wrapped in tubes and machines, but still breathing, barely.

She was weak, her voice thin, her skin pale against the white sheets. But her spirit? That was still iron. She held a small red prayer cloth in her hand, the kind sent out by Reverend Ike, the bold and booming radio preacher she listened to faithfully. She pressed that cloth against her chest as if it held her together. And repeatedly, I heard her mumble his words: *"You can't lose with the stuff I use."* To anyone else, it might've sounded like a gimmick. But to Mama, it was faith wrapped in fabric. That little cloth became her shield. Her anchor. Her daily declaration of survival.

And she survived for a time. She got stronger, talked a little more, and sat up in bed with that familiar steel in her spine.

But time has a quiet finality. You never know when the last good day is until you're looking back at it. In 1976, not long after I thought we might get a few more years together, her body surrendered. There was no loud warning. No long goodbye. Just a soft silence that came and stayed.

When she left, it wasn't just her breath that stopped. It was a chapter of my life. With her went the last piece of my childhood. The one who had held my hand through poverty, through my father's absence, through the aches of becoming a man, she was gone. And yet, something in me knew she hadn't lost. She had finished her race, prayer cloth still in hand, with faith intact and head held high.

Then, just two years after Mama passed, in 1978, I buried my father, Bates Murray. Our relationship had always been complicated, marked by more silence than words, more questions than answers. He wasn't there when I needed him, not when I was a boy, not when I was figuring out how to be a man, not when I was raising my children. I spent years walking with the weight of that absence, a quiet ache that settled into my spirit like dust on a forgotten shelf. I didn't speak on it much, but I carried it.

Yet, I stepped in when he grew old, and his mind began to unravel like a thread from a fraying coat. I did for him what he had not done for me. I arranged for his care, brought him into a local elder facility, and brought him to my house on weekends. I made sure he ate well. I watched his favorite shows with him. I listened when he mumbled through half-memories and faded names. I bathed him when the nurses couldn't. I sat beside him in stillness, sometimes praying, sometimes just breathing.

It wasn't easy. Forgiveness never is. It didn't come all at once. It came in pieces slowly, like light creeping through a cracked door. There were moments I wanted to ask my father why, why he left, why he didn't show up, why I had to find my way without him. But I never did. If God could forgive me for my flaws, I could extend the same mercy to the man who gave me life, even if he didn't provide me presence. Then came the discovery, something that shifted everything. I found a notebook in a small box tucked away in his room. Inside were poems, simple, handwritten verses in neat, deliberate script. They weren't loud or polished. They didn't rhyme perfectly. But they were honest. Tender. Thoughtful. They were quiet reflections on love, on regret, on time, and on God. The kind of words that feel like whispers from a soul that's seen some things and learned too late how to speak of them.

Reading those poems stunned me. I sat at my desk with tears welling up, page after page. I had spent a lifetime wondering where my gift for storytelling and language had come from. And now, here it was, tucked away in the spirit of the man I had both loved and resented. He hadn't shown it in hugs or fatherly advice. He hadn't spoken it through guidance or open arms. But he spoke. Through poetry. Through ink and silence. Somehow, in that discovery, I felt like I saw him for the first time.

When he died, I decided to bury him beside Mama at Saint Mark Cemetery. Not because he had been perfect. Not because we had tied up every loose end. But because he was mine. Because sometimes love isn't clean, it's just faithful. And honoring him, even with a fractured past, was the final act of peace I could offer both him and myself.

I gave him a proper funeral. The choir sang. The pastor preached. And when the dirt fell softly over his casket, it covered not just the body of a father but the ache that had followed me since boyhood.

That day, I laid to rest both the man and the wound.

And I left with one of his poems folded in my coat pocket, proof that even broken roots can still carry something beautiful.

Through it all, church anchored me. When the world felt too loud, too violent, too unpredictable, Liberty Hill CME was the quiet in my storm. We met every third Sunday, back when churches rotated pastors and pulpits, and the sanctuary didn't need chandeliers or stained glass to feel holy. The floors creaked beneath us. The ceiling fans stirred more dust than a breeze. But the Spirit of God was thick in the room. It clung to the air like heat in a summer tent revival.

Because our home church didn't meet weekly, we visited neighboring churches throughout the month, building bonds that stretched across backroads and branches. On first Sundays, we went to Truevine Baptist, where the choir could lift you from sorrow straight into praise. On second Sundays, we worshipped at Israelite Baptist, where my Uncle Clarence and Aunt Doris Hall were members, and the sermons rang out like thunder wrapped in scripture. On fourth Sundays, we sat at Hebrew Baptist, where Sarah held her membership, singing with a voice that still echoes in my memory like a balm. Each congregation had its own rhythm and fire, but all were filled with testifying, tambourines, clapping hands, and the determined love of a people trying to hold each other together in a world trying to pull us apart.

But nothing matched the fire of summer revivals. Those were sacred weeks, not just for the church but for the community's soul. Every church in the parish would take its turn hosting, from Monday to Friday night, the pews were packed, the windows open, and the air thick with sweat, perfume, and the power of the Holy Ghost. Sisters' heels tapped the wooden floors in rhythm with the choir, and you could feel the Spirit sweeping through like a gust that no man could contain.

There was the mourners' bench, a front row of sacred tension where the unsaved would sit while deacons, mothers, and seasoned saints prayed and sang around them, crying out until that soul surrendered. It wasn't a show; it was spiritual warfare, raw and honest. When someone "got saved," the whole church erupted. Some shouted. Some wept. Some just sat stunned by the weight of salvation settling on a soul.

And then, that Sunday, baptisms, not in heated pools or fiberglass tubs, but in creeks shaded by cypress and pine, where two sticks held up a white sheet over muddy water, creating a makeshift tabernacle. I watched young boys and older adults step into that water and come out trembling, cleansed, and new. That wasn't just tradition. That was holy ground.

During that time, I served as a steady and faithful deacon, the man called on to read scripture, pray over offerings, and open service with solemn devotion. I was the one who showed up early to unlock the doors and stayed late to fold chairs. People leaned on me. Trusted me. But I wasn't yet broken open by the Word of God. Not yet. I believed. I served. But I hadn't yet come to the place where the Word of God got inside me and shook me to the bone. I stood near the fire, but I hadn't stepped in.

That would come later when a loss would become too loud to silence when the call would no longer wait. When the God

I sang about on Sundays would speak directly into my bones and say, *"You're next."*

My home became a sanctuary of a different kind on the weekends, not for sermons, but for stories. It drew in the community elders, the ones time had humbled and softened. I wasn't much of a drinker, but I found comfort in their presence. There was a sacred honesty in those moments, a wisdom shared not through lectures but through laughter. The walls absorbed something more profound than words as they sat and talked, a legacy of survival, struggle, and the quiet joy of still being here.

Most Saturdays, you'd find Cousin Ivy Bates nearby, settled into a chair as he had always been part of the landscape. He was a descendant of Phyllis Cruel, our shared bloodline ran deep, and he carried himself with the quiet weight of that history. Tall and fair-skinned, with wavy hair that still hinted at the striking man he'd once been, Ivy bore the look of someone who had seen too much and spoken too little. After cancer took his wife, something in him dimmed. Grief sat in his eyes, and whiskey often hung on his breath like a second skin. He lived alone in a shotgun house perched on a hill we all called Ivy Bates Hill, a place so connected to him, it might as well have been named at birth. That house overlooked the world below with weary defiance, and Ivy did the same. When he came around, he didn't ask permission or make announcements, he just settled in, like a man returning to sacred ground. And he belonged. Always had.

Then there was Ed Moore, a red-complexioned, thin fellow with a soft shuffle in his step and hands rough from carpentry. He had helped build our house, quiet, steady, and always dependable with a hammer. But when he spoke, it was often through a haze of drink and half-slurred bravado. "I ain't very scary," he'd say, squinting with one eye, "but I will fight." His words stumbled out like they were drunk themselves, full of grit and stubborn pride. He'd sit low in his chair, arms crossed like a man ready for the world to try him. And truth be told, no one really wanted to.

And then there was Sam Lot, a jolly fellow if there ever was one. He was always grinning, always smoking a short, wet cigar that clung to his lip like it knew no other home. His eyes, glazed with years of whiskey and wide-eyed joy, sparkled like mischief in motion. Sam was a womanizer, a drinker, a fisherman, and a hunter, a man who lived fully and loudly. His laugh cracked through the air like dry wood snapping in a fire, and when he grinned, it was enchanting, like he knew a secret you'd never guess. He'd slap your back, tell a tale that only half made sense, and somehow leave you feeling better than when he found you.

They were all characters, flawed, funny, raw, and honest. And I enjoyed every single one of them. Not because they were perfect but because they were present. They reminded me that life didn't have to be polished to be beautiful.

Loggy Bayou in the 1970s was alive. The land pulsed with the rhythm of families, fields, and front porch conversations. We gathered for games on warm afternoons, softball and kickball, kids chasing each other barefoot through weeds and wildflowers. Laughter filled the air like birdsong. We were poor in pocket but rich in rhythm, laughter, and land.

I farmed hard. I plowed rows of peas, peanuts, corn, and watermelon, the sun scorching my back, sweat soaking my shirt, and soil caked into my hands like a second skin. I raised pigs, chickens, and horses and, for a season, even grew cucumbers to sell at the farmer's market. We lived off the land, and the land responded with favor.

My father-in-law, Mike Reliford, had a system passed down from men who knew how to make survival stretch into abundance. He'd pen and grain-feed a calf, then slaughter it and divide the meat among his children, steak, hamburger, liver, the whole thing. It was never fancy, but it was plentiful, honest food, and my family never went hungry. Not once.

And though I spent my weekdays teaching, I never let school end at the bell. I challenged my students and the neighborhood kids to memorize scripture and poetry, Langston Hughes's "Mother to Son" and "Dream Deferred," Maya Angelou's "Still I Rise," Kipling's "If," James Weldon Johnson's "The Creation." I poured the word and the wordsmiths into them with the same passion.

I even directed one-act plays, usually casting the bold kids in the lead and placing the shy ones where they could grow quietly. One of those plays, *Prelude to Darkness*, left a mark I won't forget. It told the story of a quiet boy named Johan, whom a young couple had adopted. The wife, Tatiana, was nurturing and full of grace, while the husband, Sebastian, was proud, set in his way, and hardened by life's disappointments.

Johan wasn't troubled, just tender. Sensitive. He loved to sketch, sing, and explore the arts. But Sebastian didn't know what to do with a boy like that. He viewed art as weakness and emotion as something to suppress. In a moment of rage and misunderstanding, Sebastian struck the boy, so hard that it temporarily blinded him. That act of violence marked a turning point. Tatiana, no longer silent, rose to Johan's defense with a ferocity that shook the stage and the audience. She confronted Sebastian not just as a wife, but as a protector and moral compass, forcing him to face the damage his pride had caused.

Ultimately, the play wasn't about blindness, it was about seeing. Sebastian had to confront himself, strip away his fear, and start learning what love truly looked like. It was a tough story, but the kind that sticks with people.

We first staged it in the school auditorium with my students, and later, I brought it to life again in churches with my children and others from the surrounding community. I remember watching them step into those roles and bring them to life with a kind of raw courage. One girl who had barely spoken in class found her voice as Tatiana, and she roared. A quiet young boy played Johan with such heartbreaking stillness that it moved the room. By the final scene, you could hear people crying in the audience. I knew then that this was more than just a school play. It was a mirror. It was a lesson. And I was proud to have helped tell it in the classroom and the community.

We'd work in the garden by day and rehearse at night, children reciting lines under the fading light while fireflies blinked their approval from the bushes. And when they got it right, when they embraced the challenge, I'd load them all into my green pickup truck, the bed filled with kids and promise, and drive them into Bossier City. We went skating. It wasn't just fun; it was a reward, a celebration. It was movement, laughter, and dignity rolling forward on wheels.

We were living well, eating well too. Not rich, but full. My wife Sarah worked tirelessly to make it all stretch and hold. She took shifts at the sewing factory, taught school during the week, and came home to a house full of never-ending life. Her father, a master carpenter, built her a beauty shop right in our yard, and on weekends, she turned it into a small business. While she styled hair inside, our children played outside, their laughter rising through the hum of the hairdryer and the aroma of pressing oil.

I'd join her in that same shop, cutting the hair of men who didn't trust just anybody with clippers. Ed Moore, Ivy Bates, and others from the porch crowd, they'd ease into my chair, settle back, and start talking about the old days while I went to work. I never went to barber school, but I'd picked up the trade back in college, cutting heads between classes to make a little money. What started as a side hustle became a skill I took pride in. I had perfected the craft the way a lot of us did, by watching. My older brother Lee had a shop up in Chicago, and I used to stand off to the side, soaking it all in. Every flick of his wrist, every clean fade, every slow drag of the straight razor, I studied it like scripture. And over time, I mastered it. Not on paper, but in practice. In the feel of the blade, in the trust of the man in the chair. We weren't just building a life. We were building a legacy, one Saturday haircut, one backyard garden, one Bible verse at a time.

And when summer break came, I'd shine up my red Ford LTD until it gleamed like a badge of honor. I'd check the tires, load the trunk with suitcases, snacks, and Sarah's pound cake wrapped in foil, and hit the road with my family. That car was more than transportation; it was a chariot carrying us into something better. We'd drive across state lines with gospel music pouring through the speakers and the windows rolled halfway down to catch the scent of pine, pavement, and possibility.

We made our way to Los Angeles, where my brother, Bates Jr., and Aunt Helen greeted us with hugs and hot plates, their home filled with laughter and the rich smells of something always simmering on the stove. Then we drove down the California coast to San Diego, where my sisters, Katherine and Clifford, welcomed us with open arms, the ocean breeze brushing against our faces like a promise that life had turned a corner. Sometimes, we'd head north to Chicago, where my brother Lee stood behind his barber's chair like a king in his kingdom. Each visit felt like a reunion with hope itself.

Every trip reminded me how far we'd come. We were a long way from scrubbing with lye soap in the backyard wash pot, from bathing babies in basins, from hauling water from a well. We were a long way from where we had come from. And I thank God for that. I thank Him for every mile traveled, every meal shared, every laugh around those kitchen tables.

Because the 1970s tried to take everything, they came for our elders, our peace, and our dignity. They came with loss and with silence, with government shifts and social storms. In that single decade, I laid to rest the three who shaped the very soil beneath my feet.

Papa, Alfred Daniels, was the anchor of our family, the quiet strength in a worn work hat, the man who taught me to plow straight rows and pray on bent knees. He left behind more than land, he left a legacy rooted in dignity. Then came the passing of my mother, Lucille Daniels Murray. She had been both shield and shelter, a woman who stitched brokenness into beauty with nothing more than grit, grace, and the word of God. And though my relationship with my father, Bates Murray, was complicated by absence and silence, I still held his poetry in my blood. I buried him, too, beside my mother, carrying not only grief but forgiveness into that sacred ground.

Their deaths left a stillness in me, an aching hush that only faith could speak into. I thought of the scripture: *"Precious in the sight of the Lord is the death of His saints."* (Psalm 116:15). And I believed it, even as the pews emptied and the dinner tables grew quieter. These weren't just losses, they were homegoings. Transitions from labor to reward. From struggle to glory.

And yet, we never stopped giving, to each other, to the land, to the Lord. We gave with calloused hands and open hearts, with tired backs and stubborn hope. Because that's what they taught us. And somehow, through storms and sorrow, through funerals and footraces, we not only survived. We thrived. And we are still here. Not because we were unshaken but because we were rooted.

BROKEN TO BE MADE WHOLE IN THE 80s

By the time the 1980s rolled around, I had walked through more than most men ever talk about, war and segregation, integration and injustice, the births of my children, and the deaths of my parents. I had taught Black children in Jim Crow classrooms, picked cotton under Southern suns, built a home nail by nail, and fought to keep my family fed, educated, and whole. I had been a soldier, a student, a teacher, a father, and a husband. Strong in body, rooted in community, but something deeper in me was stirring. A crack had started to run down the middle of my soul. Not to break me apart but to let something greater in.

In 1980, I turned fifty-one. My children were growing up fast. Kendell had joined the Army, Jackie, and Roy Jr. were in college, and Patrick wasn't far behind. Sarah and I had spent decades raising our family with routine and reverence. We had built a life, solid, predictable, God-fearing. But I had not yet been broken open by the Word. I was a deacon at

Liberty Hill CME, present every third Sunday, faithful in service. But faith isn't always forged in comfort. Sometimes, it takes a holy fire to melt the iron walls around a man's heart.

In 1985, after twenty-seven years in education, I retired from the Red River Parish school system. Integration had reshaped the classroom. Many of my coworkers were now my former students. Even the principal was once one of my pupils. The torch was ready to be passed. I had given my best to teaching, and the classroom had given me back decades of purpose. But I knew God was calling me to something more profound. At first, I thought retirement would be a season of rest, a time to breathe, to reflect, and to enjoy the fruits of decades spent teaching, guiding, and serving. But peace didn't come easy. Not long after filing my retirement papers in 1985, I received a letter that felt like a slap. The retirement office had mishandled my paperwork, and just like that, the teaching system denied my health benefits.

After nearly thirty years of faithful service to the Red River Parish School System, teaching Black and White students, leading through integration, and mentoring future leaders, I was left uncovered. No insurance. No explanation. No apology. That betrayal cut deep. It wasn't just the loss of a benefit, it was the loss of dignity. I had paid my dues. I had done my part. But the system still found a way to leave me exposed.

And yet, God doesn't leave His people unprotected.

While the world said no, God redirected my steps. I remembered I was a veteran, a soldier who had stood watch in Alaska, braved snowfields in the Korean War era, and proudly served this country. I turned to the Veterans Health Administration, and it was there, through the VA, that I found my covering. The same uniform that once weighed on my shoulders now became a shield. Through the VA, I received medical care, check-ups, and the kind of support that reminded me I was not forgotten.

God has a way of using what man mishandles. That season of rejection opened the door for something sacred. Around that time, I reconnected with my old principal from Grand Bayou, Mr. P.L. Buggs, a towering figure in my early career who had once led with quiet strength and fairness. Now retired and recently widowed, he had traded his grade books for a Bible, stepping into ministry as pastor of a small, spirit-filled church called Israelite.

What began as a few friendly visits quickly became something more profound. Mr. Buggs was grieving, and I was searching. And somewhere between shared silence and long drives, God did His work. I became his driver, his quiet companion on the road to Dallas revivals, family gatherings, hospital visits, and funerals. He'd sit in the passenger seat of that deep burgundy Cadillac, talking in calm tones that somehow steadied us both.

He never preached at me. He didn't need to. Watching how he moved through sorrow gracefully and led with humility began to stir something in me. I had seen preachers who wore their titles like crowns, but Mr. Buggs wore his calling like a mantle. Sacred. Steady. Still.

Each journey with him asked me new questions: What if this is your next assignment? What if all your years in the classroom were training for a higher purpose? What if ministry isn't behind a pulpit, but beside a person, walking quietly toward God?

I didn't know it yet, but the road to ministry had already begun, and it started behind the wheel of a Cadillac, beside a grieving pastor, carrying more than just a man. I was carrying the seeds of my own surrender.

But it wasn't until I encountered Clemmie and Hosea Townson that the real breaking began, not the kind that destroys but reveals what's buried deep in the soul. Clemmie was a former classmate of Sarah's, a woman of quiet elegance and deep conviction who had spent years in California before returning home to Ringgold. She and her husband Hosea settled into a sturdy brick home nestled on a vast, hundred-acre stretch of land, and they brought with them not just financial stability but spiritual overflow. God had blessed them; more importantly, they believed in sharing those blessings.

Clemmie approached Sarah and me one afternoon and said, "We're doing something different. We're going in." I didn't know what she meant. She smiled, that kind of knowing smile that comes from someone who has spent time in both battle and prayer. "We're holding a shut-in," she said. "You and Sarah ought to come."

I agreed without fully understanding. At the time, I had never fasted in my life, not once. I had always known the Word, respected the Word, and even taught the Word, but I had never denied my flesh to hear God clearer. I had never laid down my comforts to seek the face of the Lord with nothing but hunger and hope in my hands. But I went.

That first shut-in was held at Mason Temple Church of God in Christ in Memphis, Tennessee, a holy place thick with the legacy of saints, prophets, and broken men made whole. That church had been built on the bones of revival, the voices of women who moaned prayers from their bellies, and the men who stomped the floorboards with conviction. It was sacred ground, where Dr. King had given his last sermon, and the echo of that final "I've been to the mountaintop" still lingered in the walls like a warning and a promise.

We arrived on a Wednesday evening, the sun low, the sky soft with early twilight. We stayed through Sunday, but the atmosphere shifted from the moment we walked through those doors. You could feel it in your bones, in your breath. It was thick with spirit, almost heavy. It didn't take long to know this was no ordinary church service. This service was spiritual surgery. We fasted. We prayed. We shouted. We cried. We fell silent and let the presence of God settle in like a holy fog. For three days straight, I didn't eat a single bite.

No meat. No bread. Just water. Just prayer, scripture, and tears. At one point, I stepped outside the sanctuary, needing air more than food. Hosea found me leaning against the wall, eyes closed, nose in the air. "You alright, Roy?" he asked. I opened my eyes, looked at him, and said, "I smell chicken." We laughed, deep and hard, but I was serious. My stomach was crying out, but deeper still, my soul was hungrier.

That shut-in broke me. Broke the man I thought I was. Broke the walls I didn't even know I had built. I cried like a child, from a place so deep I hadn't touched it in decades. I confessed things I had buried. I repented with a tongue heavy from silence. I lay prostrate on that church floor and let the tears fall like rain. And God, gracious, merciful, waiting God, He met me there.

I had been in church all my life. But I had never felt God like that. I had never heard Him as clearly as I did when, somewhere in the stillness between scripture and sobbing, Isaiah 6:8 rose in my spirit: *"Whom shall I send, and who will go for us?"* And from the pit of my belly, without hesitation, I whispered, *"Here am I. Send me."*

That was the moment. Not the day I became a preacher, but the day I became a man on fire. Something turned inside me. Something opened. The Word wasn't just something I read, it became something I carried. Something I breathed. Something I began to speak with boldness but not with performance. I didn't want to be one of those loud preachers who needed an organ to back them up. I wanted to teach. I wanted to instruct. I wanted to reveal the power of the Word for what it is, transformative, living, enough. And in that fire, in that awakening, God began leading me deeper into ministry. What started as teaching and testimony would eventually grow into something greater, my call to pastor.

I started teaching like the Word mattered, not just in Sunday school but in my home, the garden, the barbershop chair, and casual conversations with young men trying to find their way. I saw ministry not just as what happens behind the pulpit but as what happens wherever you show up with truth in your mouth and love in your heart.

After many years of serving faithfully as a deacon and as a Sunday school teacher, the Lord saw fit to call me higher. It was in the late 1980s that I was asked to pastor Liberty Hill CME Church, the very church that had shaped my childhood and anchored my early faith. That place was holy ground to me. I had grown up within its walls, sung hymns with my family in those wooden pews, and watched the sunlight fall in slanted beams through its tall windows. The pulpit, once so distant and mysterious to me as a boy, now stood before me as a place of responsibility and reverence. To pastor Liberty Hill, it was not just an assignment, it was a homecoming, a sacred return to the soil that had raised me.

But as I began to lead, I also began to discern a quiet struggle, one not born of malice but of neglect and fatigue. Like many traditional denominations, the CME church was stretched thin across generations and geographies, trying to meet the needs of both city congregations and rural churches like ours. Yet in that effort, it seemed the smaller country churches were often left waiting, waiting for resources, waiting for support, waiting to be seen. We sent in our tithes and participated in the connectional system, but what came back to our community felt limited. The spirit of Liberty Hill remained strong, but the infrastructure was aging, and the challenges of sustaining a small rural congregation weighed heavily on my heart. I began to wonder if there might be a different path, not away from God but closer to His people.

I carried that question in my spirit for months. I prayed in the quiet of early mornings and in the stillness of midnight. I sought the Lord in scripture, in silence, and in long walks through the woods behind my home. What kept rising in me was a call to serve more directly and flexibly, to meet the needs of our people without waiting on a broader system that, through no fault of its own, couldn't always reach us in time. So, with a heart full of peace and a clear word from

God, I made the decision to step away from the denomination, not in protest, but in pursuit of purpose. And with that, Liberty Hill Outreach was born.

We didn't have the security of a denomination behind us, nor the polish of a large sanctuary or an overflowing treasury. What we had was conviction. What we had was calling. And what we had was each other. My wife, Sarah, stood beside me with quiet courage. She left Hebrew Baptist, the church her family had cherished for generations, and joined me in building something new. That was no small act. It takes a deep faith to walk away from your spiritual birthplace and follow your husband into uncharted territory. But Sarah did it with grace and determination, trusting not just in me but in the God who had called us both.

Together, we rebuilt Liberty Hill not with bricks and beams but with trust, testimony, and tireless service. There were no chandeliers or colored glass, no organ lofts or marble floors. But what we had was honest worship. We had a community that showed up with casseroles, questions, and quiet hope. And what we had, more than anything, was the presence of God. People came not because we were grand but because we were grounded. They came to hear a Word that met them where they were, whether in grief, in doubt, in transition, or in thanksgiving.

There were days when the offering plate came back almost empty, and there were nights when I wondered if I had made a mistake. But every time I felt weary, I would think about the men and women who built churches out of brush arbors, who met under trees and in kitchens and believed that God could move in humble places. I would remember my mother's words, words that had followed me through every storm and season: "He brought us from disgrace to God's amazing grace, and I don't believe He brought us this far to leave us." That saying, passed down like an heirloom of faith, became my anchor. And in those moments when the pews were few and the weight was heavy, I would lean on that promise and keep going.

Liberty Hill Outreach wasn't just a church. It was a rebirth. It was a reminder that ministry doesn't depend on title or tradition, it depends on obedience. And even now, when I think back to those early days, I see not the struggle but the fruit. I see families restored, young people baptized, and elders who found peace after years of searching. We may not have had much, but we had enough. And in the hands of God, enough becomes abundance.

Even as Liberty Hill Outreach took root, our spiritual walk deepened. For the next few years, once a month, Sarah and I traveled with Clemmie and Hosea to shut-ins across the region, small storefront churches, borrowed sanctuaries, and old tents pitched on borrowed land. We fasted. We prayed. We slept on church pews, laid our faces on cold tile floors, and lifted our hands toward heaven, even when they trembled. And in those sacred spaces, between hymns and hunger, between silence and surrender, I was made new.

By the end of the '80s, my children were standing on the threshold of adulthood, beginning to shape lives of their own. Kendell was serving in the Army, learning discipline under a different flag, while Jackie, Roy Jr., and Patrick were still in college, stretching their minds and finding their footing in a world that didn't always welcome them with open arms. They were becoming, becoming thinkers, doers, believers, and dreamers. I had done my part: laid down the rails of discipline, anchored them in scripture, and wrapped them in the quiet strength of Sarah's prayers. They had seen hard work done with dignity, love given without limits, and faith lived out loud. My role was shifting now. I had to step back and let God take the lead, trusting that the seeds we had sown would grow in His time. And let me tell you, that kind of trust? It's a different kind of hard.

Also, in the 1980s, my heart found a resting place in Los Angeles, where my beloved Aunt Helen, Mama's sister, was still living. She was a piece of home away from home. Aunt Helen was sharp, stylish, and full of heart. After her husband, Uncle Dick, passed away, she leaned on me the way elders do when grief turns the house quiet. I began spending more time out there, especially in the summers, flying in from Louisiana and trading the scent of pine for the sunshine of Southern California.

She had a new Buick, silver, smooth, and shining like something blessed, and she trusted me with the keys. I'd drive it all over L.A., picking up cousins, visiting old friends, and cruising through streets lined with palm trees and movie marquees. We'd ride to Watts and Inglewood, sometimes just to get lunch and talk about the old days, the days of Liberty Hill, Mama and Clifford, Papa, and the porch in Loggy Bayou. She became more than an aunt, she was a mother in spirit, a friend in faith, and my safe place in the West.

Back home in Ringgold, my wife Sarah was still holding it down, faithfully, gracefully, and without complaint. She kept working hard, still doing hair in the beauty shop her father had built with his own hands, just steps from our back door. That little shop had become more than a place for curls and presses, it was a hub, a place of therapy and testimony, where women came not just to be styled but to be seen and heard. You could always hear laughter through the screen door, smell the burnt hair from a hot comb, and catch pieces of scripture and encouragement between conversations about family and faith.

Meanwhile, I was still in my rhythm, cutting hair for the old-timers out in the yard or in the back room, keeping the tradition alive even as the faces changed. By the early '80s, Ed Moore and Ivy Bates had both gone on, but their memory still sat heavy in the chair. I could almost hear Ed's slurred sass, *"I ain't very scary, but I will fight"*, or see Ivy settling in, nodding like he'd heard the joke before but still appreciated the telling. The newer folks came not just for the trim but for the fellowship. I'd pour a glass of water, wipe off the chair, and sharpen my clippers while they filled the room with stories, some fresh, some passed down, all of them laced with truth and laughter. The shop echoed with memories, with the ghosts of good men, with old wisdom and a little bit of trash talk while the smell of supper drifted in from the house, reminding us all we were home.

Our home never quieted down. It stayed lively with laughter, layered with prayer, and scented with love, beans on the stove, cornbread in the oven, greens simmering in a big pot, and gospel music humming low in the background. The door stayed open, and the table stayed set. Folks came through for a word, a haircut, or just to sit in the peace for a while.

We were still farming, raising chickens and hogs, and working the land with faith and calloused hands. Our garden fed more than our bodies, it fed the community, our pride, and our souls.

And in all of that, the routine, the joy, the labor, the laughter, the 1980s whispered a lesson that became a pillar in my life: You can serve your family. You can serve your church. You can serve your community with full hands and an open heart. But until God breaks you, truly breaks you, you haven't yet begun to live your purpose.

I had spent years teaching history, shaping minds with dates and names, with stories of struggle and survival. But now, I was being called to something more. Now, I was ready to teach truth, to walk in the light, to lead not with a raised voice but with a quiet, rooted peace. Not just to preach but to pastor. Not just to speak, but to listen, to shepherd, to follow the Spirit wherever it led. I was broken. But not to be discarded. I was broken to be made whole. And that breaking, that sacred undoing, prepared me for everything that came next.

WE'VE COME THIS FAR BY FAITH:

THE 1990S

The 1990s were a decade of reflection, of reckoning. I had lived through the unthinkable and somehow still stood on two feet. Segregation and integration, war and poverty, backbreaking labor and righteous battles, the raising of four children, and the burying of both my parents. I had watched history happen, and I had helped make it in many ways. By now, I wasn't just living, I was testifying. And the years I carried on my back didn't weigh me down. They crowned me. I felt the heaviness not as a burden but as a mantle. God had preserved me, not just for survival, but for purpose.

By 1990, my season of shut-ins with Clemmie and Hosea Townson was coming to a close. For many powerful, soul-stripping years, we had prayed through the night, fasted for days, and lay on cold church floors with our hands stretched toward heaven. Those years were sacred. We surrendered everything, flesh, pride, fear, ego, and let the Holy Spirit break us into something new. I had been remade in those shut-ins, humbled to dust, and reshaped in fire. I thought that was the final surrender. But I was wrong. A new battle was already forming, this time in my own body.

It started with a routine visit to the VA hospital. Nothing felt particularly off; it was just a regular checkup. But then the nurse called me back, her eyes too careful, her voice too polite. They took blood, ran tests, and made small talk. And then came the moment, the one that carved itself into memory like a blade. The doctor entered the room, sat across from me, and spoke the words I didn't know I was waiting to fear. "Mr. Murray," he said, clipboard in hand, "the biopsy returned positive." The room went still. The walls were beige, but they turned cold. The fluorescent light above my head flickered slightly, and I remember hearing the distant hum of the air vent like it was the only sound left in the world. "Cancer," he continued. "Prostate." His words came slow and heavy like bricks being stacked on my chest. I tried to nod. Tried to act like I understood. But I didn't. Not really. I heard it but didn't feel it until I got to the parking lot and sat alone in my car. And then the weight landed. Cancer. After all, I'd been through. After everything I had overcome. They sent me through a whirlwind of appointments, blood draws, MRIs, consultations with specialists who talked to me like I was already halfway gone. The treatments came next. Hormone therapy to slow the cancer's growth. Cryotherapy, machines that would freeze the tumors in my body like they were trying to stop death mid-step. I listened, I nodded, and I signed the papers. But inside, my spirit rose with one truth: I would need more than machines to be healed. I would need God.

Not long after that diagnosis, we gathered for one of our final shut-in revivals. I was frail, the fire in my bones cooled by fear and fatigue. But I showed up. I lay there, prostrated before the Lord, body aching, stomach empty, spirit burning. And somewhere in the middle of that sanctuary, between the hymns and hallelujahs, between the groans of the faithful and the whisper of angels, I broke down.

I wept. Not like a grown man. Like a child. My tears hit the floor in rhythm with my heartbeat. I could feel the hands of the saints resting gently on my back, pressing faith into my shoulders. And there, in the sacred silence that only exists between desperation and deliverance, I whispered a prayer from the deepest part of me: "Lord, You've brought me through too much to leave me here."

And I meant it. I laid that cancer on the altar, cell by cell, fear by fear. I didn't ask for a miracle. I just asked for more time. More years. More purpose. And what I got was something no doctor could guarantee: healing. Not remission. Not partial. Healing. From that day forward, I've never had another problem with it. Not one. No recurrence. No complications. No residue of that diagnosis was left in my body. God didn't just stop the cancer, He erased it.

That wasn't the doctor's doing. That wasn't the cryo machine. That was God. That shut-in became my upper room. That sanctuary became my hospital. And those prayers became my medicine. I walked in weak. But I walked out whole. And I knew, more clearly than ever before, God was not done with me yet.

By the end of the 1990s, all four of my children had settled into their rhythm, grown, grounded, and walking their own paths in a world still learning to honor Black brilliance. Kendell had completed his time in the Army and brought that same discipline into a career in information technology. He joined Roy Jr., who was also thriving in the information technology field out in Dallas. Patrick was finishing up college at my beloved alma mater, Grambling, while Jackie had found her stride in accounting, building a steady career in Shreveport with the same quiet focus and grace she had carried since childhood. She hadn't started a family yet, but her life was whole and forward-moving. They were no longer children under my roof, they were adults in their own right, each shaped by the love, prayers, and lessons Sarah and I had poured into them like seeds into the soil.

Looking at the lives they were building, I knew I hadn't been perfect. But I had been faithful. I had given them more than what I had been given: a home rooted in faith, an expectation of excellence, and the dignity to walk into any room as if they belonged there. I hadn't just raised them to survive. I had raised them to stand with their heads high, their backs straight, and their souls anchored in something more substantial than fear.

Even with my children grown and gone, I stayed busy. Retirement had given me rest once before, but rest wasn't what I needed now. Purpose doesn't retire. I returned to teaching part-time because I still had lessons left to give, lessons from textbooks and life. I had walked through fire and came out still able to speak. And I believed that kind of testimony belonged not just in pulpits but in classrooms, hallways, and hearts.

But even when I wasn't behind a desk, I was still teaching. I was ministering, in barber chairs with the older men who needed more than a haircut, in church pews with those who were hungry for a word, at kitchen tables where the family gathered, and out in the garden rows where sweat and scripture often mingled in the same soil. I sowed seeds, both literal and spiritual, and watched them grow in children, neighbors, and friends who came for okra but left with wisdom. My hands stayed busy. My mind stayed sharp.

And my heart? It stayed fixed on God. Because even then, I knew, my best days weren't behind me. They were still unfolding.

One of the greatest joys of the 1990s, a true crown on that season of my life, was my work with the Ringgold Alumni Association. In the wake of integration, when the dust settled, and the school boards had done their work, our Black schools were gone. Not just closed, but erased. Our elementary schools, our junior highs, our high schools, buildings that once rang with our laughter and carried our dreams were either repurposed into offices or left to rot, their bricks crumbling like broken promises. But what they couldn't close was the legacy. They couldn't repurpose our memory. They couldn't bulldoze the fire we still carried in our bones. Integration may have dissolved the structures, but it didn't destroy the village. And that's what the Ringgold Alumni Association was all about, rebuilding that village, one hug, one memory, one sacred reunion at a time.

We started small. A few phone calls. A few potlucks. A flyer in the mail. But then it spread, like revival fire. From Louisiana to Texas, Chicago to Los Angeles, classmates began to emerge like seeds after rain. Men and women who had once walked barefoot down red dirt roads to reach segregated schools were now flying across the country in tailored suits and Sunday-best dresses, determined to reconnect. We gathered in banquet halls, church basements, community centers, and even under open skies, wherever there was room for joy. And when we met, something beautiful happened. Time folded. People who hadn't seen one another since the 1950s and '60s fell into each other's arms as no years had passed. There was laughter, deep, belly-shaking laughter. There were tears, the kind that cleanse the heart. There was testimony. And music. And spirit. We weren't just telling stories. We were resurrecting something holy.

I didn't take the position lightly when I was elected President of the Ringgold Alumni Association. I knew it wasn't just a title, it was a ministry. We weren't just organizing reunions. We were preserving memory. We were honoring our elders. We were lighting torches for those who would come next. This movement wasn't just nostalgia. This movement was legacy work.

In 1994, as we prepared for our fifth alumni gathering, I sat at my desk with a Bible in front of me and a blank sheet of paper. I prayed over every word I would write. I knew it had to be more than an opening message, it needed to be a call to arms, a spiritual anchor. That message opened with these words:

"The Lord has allowed us to come together one more time. We welcome you from various cities and towns across this nation. This fifth alumni reunion is dedicated to those who bore their burdens in the heat of the day. Now it's our responsibility to give wings to dreams because we must keep hope alive."

That wasn't just poetic. It was prophetic.

Because we were watching something painful unfold, our young people were slipping away. Pulled by the streets, swayed by false promises, distracted by a world that no longer taught them who they were. Morals were unraveling. Church pews were emptying. Neighborhoods were dimming. We couldn't afford to just gather, grill ribs, and dance to Sam Cooke. No, we had to build something lasting. We turned the Ringgold Alumni Association into a bridge, not just between classmates but between generations. We built scholarship funds. We shared testimonies. We honored those who came before us and challenged those coming after us. And in that work, we kept the spirit of Liberty Hill, of Grand Bayou, of Ringgold Color High, alive. We weren't just keeping in touch. We were keeping the story alive. We were keeping the fire lit. And we were reminding our people that though the schools may have closed, our legacy had only just begun.

Even into the 1990s, I kept finding my way back to what felt familiar. And nothing was more familiar, or more grounding, than visiting my Aunt Helen in Los Angeles.

By then, Aunt Helen was in her eighties and still sharper than ever. She kept a new Buick parked out front like clockwork, always top of the line, smooth-riding, clean inside and out.

She wasn't flashy, just steady. Every time I came to visit, she'd toss me the keys with a smirk, like I was still that country boy trying to find his way. I'd drive that car all over L.A., Crenshaw, Inglewood, Long Beach, visiting family, catching up with old friends, or just cruising those wide California boulevards with the sun on my face and freedom in my bones.

We had a rhythm, Aunt Helen and I. We'd sit at her kitchen table sipping coffee, surrounded by the smell of collard greens and sweet potato pie. She didn't talk much unless she had something to say, but when she did, you listened. And you laughed. That woman had fire in her tongue and gold in her heart. She'd say things that would catch you off guard, make you think, and make you chuckle all in the same breath.

One of her favorite pastimes was gambling. She loved it. I'd drive her all the way to Las Vegas, just the two of us, her in her oversized sunglasses, purse clutched in her lap, ready for the slots. But Aunt Helen had a saying that always made me smile. Before she played, she'd glance over and say, "It ain't gambling if you don't pop your finger." And the truth was, she never did. She never snapped her fingers, never made a fuss. To her, popping your finger meant you were *really* gambling, tempting luck, chasing something. But if you sat there cool and calm and pressed the button without any flourish, you weren't gambling. Not really. There is no sin in it. Just passing the time. That was Aunt Helen's gospel.

As the years passed and she moved into her late nineties, I kept coming back. Not just out of duty, but because being around her felt like peace. Like slipping into a memory that still had room for the present. Even as my own life changed, retirement, grandchildren, ministry, Aunt Helen remained a steady hum beneath it all. She saw me. She remembered me. She made me feel like I still mattered.

That kind of love doesn't die. It lives in the smell of cornbread, in the shine of a clean Buick, in a quiet casino ride down the I-15. It lives in memory, in legacy, and in laughter.

Some folks fade from your life. But Aunt Helen? She stayed. And even now, when I pass a casino or hear the hum of a Buick's engine, I can still hear her voice, steady and full of knowing: *"It ain't gambling if you don't pop your finger."* And just like that, I smile, and I remember.

When she passed in the early 2000s, it felt like another part of my childhood was laid to rest. But even in her absence, she had one more lesson to teach me. In her will, she left me something, a gift I never asked for, never expected. I don't speak of it often, not because it wasn't meaningful, but because what mattered more was what it represented. That small inheritance was a reminder that God sees your heart, even when the world overlooks you. The quiet things you do in love, the prayers, the phone calls, the visits, the patience, matter in heaven's record book. Her gift wasn't just money. It was honor, memory, and love that lingered past the grave.

Back home in Ringgold, life settled into a steady, familiar rhythm, a rhythm made of faith, family, and good, honest work. My wife Sarah still did her clients' hair in the little beauty shop. On any given weekend, you could hear the soft hum of her blow dryer, smell the press and curl warming on the stove, and hear the women laughing and catching up on life. That shop wasn't just a business, it was a sanctuary. A place where women came to feel beautiful, seen, and heard. And Sarah had the gift. She could make a woman feel like a queen just by carefully parting her hair.

And me? I was still cutting hair now and then, just not like I used to. By the '90s, most of the old-timers had passed on. Ed Moore and Ivy Bates were long gone, but their names still floated through conversations on the porch, their stories living on in laughter and long pauses. The clippers didn't hum as often, and the line of waiting chairs had thinned out. But every now and then, someone would stop by, an old friend, a neighbor needing a trim, or just somebody looking for company, and I'd dust off the chair and get to work. Cutting hair was my ministry. That chair had been my pulpit for years. And even as the clippers grew quiet, it still connected me to the people, one head, and one story, at a time.

I was still farming, but not like before. I'd stopped raising livestock, no more pigs in the pen or chickens in the yard. All my children were grown and gone, building lives of their own. But I kept the garden going. Peas, sweet potatoes, okra, corn, and watermelons still came up out of that soil, just like they always had. We didn't cook as much from the garden anymore, but the harvest never went to waste. Whatever I picked, I gave away, to neighbors, church folks, or anyone who could use it. By then, we relied more on the grocery store, but my connection to the land hadn't left me. That garden was no longer just for feeding my own family, it was an offering. A reminder that life had been generous to me, and it was my turn to be gracious in return.

By the end of the 1990s, I could feel something settling in my soul, a kind of peace. I had lived long enough to watch the promises of God unfold in my life. I had seen the seeds I planted in my children bloom tall and proud. I had watched the wisdom of my elders, once whispered in the fields and on front porches, now echo through the lives of the next generation.

The 1990s taught me that faith isn't just about what you believe; it's about what you build. Day by day, brick by brick, prayer by prayer, you build a family, a community, and a life that honors God.

And as I sat on my porch some evenings, clippers in one hand and a glass of sweet tea in the other, I could look out over the land and say with a complete heart: We made it. And we're still building.

STILL MARCHING IN POWER (2000–2019)

The turn of the century didn't slow me down, it simply redirected my energy. The world had crossed into the new millennium, clocks ticked past Y2K without the collapse we were warned to expect, and technology began moving faster than most of us could chase. But while the rest of the world was looking at their computers, holding their breath to see if the digital age would betray them, I was still listening to a different kind of ticking, not the one in my watch, but the one in my spirit.

I felt purpose pulsing like a second heartbeat. That inner rhythm, the one that had carried me through cotton fields, classrooms, pulpits, shut-ins, and barbershops, was still alive and steady. I had been teaching since Eisenhower was president, back when schools were still legally segregated, and Black teachers were paid less for doing more. I had stood in front of chalkboards before seat belts were standard, before calculators replaced long division, and before students had screens in their hands instead of pencils. I had written lesson plans with my sleeves rolled up and sweat on my brow, and even now, after all those decades, I still rose each morning with the instinct to teach.

From 2000 to 2003, I remained in the classroom, working part-time, not because I had to, but because I still had more to give. Teaching had never been a job to me. It was a calling. A ministry. A sacred trust. I didn't show up just to clock in, I showed up to build a nation, one student at a time. Each lesson plan was more than curriculum, it was a brick. Each child was more than a name on a roster, they were a seed full of potential, waiting for someone to believe in them enough to water the soil.

The education system was shifting all around me. Standards changed. Language changed. Tools changed. But my purpose remained the same. As computers replaced typewriters and classrooms grew quieter under the glow of tablets and smartboards, I still found my place in it, planting wisdom in rows, just like I once planted peas and okra in red clay soil. There was something timeless about that act: pouring knowledge into someone and watching them grow. But in 2003, I finally put down my chalk for good. I walked out of the classroom, not with regret, but with gratitude. Over four decades of service had earned me the right to sit down. But not to stop. Never to stop. Because when purpose is in your bones, retirement is just another chapter. It's not the end of your work, just the beginning of a new assignment.

By that time, all of my children had graduated from college and were stepping fully into the lives we had prayed for. Roy Jr., Kendell, and Patrick had all settled in Dallas, Texas, three brothers, each building their legacy in a city far from the red clay roads of Loggy Bayou. Kendell had married and was raising two beautiful children of his own. Jackie was still living in Shreveport with her husband and had started a family. I looked at them with awe, four Black children who had once sat at my kitchen table doing homework, now grown with degrees, careers, and children of their own. They fulfilled every whispered prayer, every verse I made them memorize, every sacrifice Sarah and I ever made.

Around that time, another chapter of my life began to unfold, one I never saw coming but one that brought both reflection and redemption. I reconnected with Ricky Roy Murray. At first, it was just a phone call. Awkward. Careful. We danced around the edges of what was unsaid, years of distance, questions unasked, emotions unspoken. But one call turned into another. Then another. Each conversation peeling back a layer. He wasn't just a voice on the other end of the line, he was a grown man living in Dallas like his brothers, raising his own family.

There were no angry confrontations, no shouting matches, just the quiet ache of time lost and the tentative hope of time reclaimed. He began visiting. At first, just once or twice, almost like he wasn't sure he belonged. But the visits grew more frequent. He'd bring his wife, and I could see the life he had built, the love, the responsibility, the fatherhood. It moved me. I didn't need a DNA test to tell me what I already knew in my spirit. I looked at him and saw myself, my mannerisms, my jawline, my eyes. Blood or not, I accepted him as mine.

That wasn't easy. It meant facing parts of myself I had locked away. It meant admitting there were chapters I hadn't read, even in my own story. But God softened my heart. Love made room. And in time, so did I. We built something honest, not perfect, but real. A relationship. A connection. A bridge across years of silence. And it became one of the quiet blessings of my later years: the chance to make peace with Ricky and myself.

I should have been satisfied. But something stirred in me. Retirement didn't mean rest. Not for me. I didn't trade lesson plans for fishing poles. I stepped deeper into my other calling: preaching, pastoring, and proclaiming. I began speaking more frequently at churches, schools, community centers, anywhere that would have me. And when February came around, my calendar stayed full. Black History Month became my platform, my pulpit, my battlefield. Because I knew that the stories we carried, the ones scarred into our DNA, could heal and empower a new generation if only they were told right.

I spoke of *Phyllis Cruel*, my great-grandmother, born in bondage in 1835. I told of how she bore five children by her slave master and walked off that plantation in Virginia with nothing but her children and the name of the man who had owned her. I shared how she found freedom, remarried, and settled in Louisiana and how, from her womb, came lineages of farmers, fighters, and freedom-seekers.

I told students in Ringgold and Coushatta about dusty fields turned into classrooms, about the long walk to school in shoes worn thin, about sitting on church pews that doubled as desks. I told them about what it meant to be "Mr. Civics" before Black teachers were respected in White schools, about standing firm when they wanted to reduce me to just "Murray" while calling others "Mister." And I told them that they were descendants of kings and queens, not criminals and statistics. I told them our people built this country brick by bloody brick and that their ancestors had survived the Middle Passage, Jim Crow, the crack epidemic, and the sting of being ignored by history books. I reminded them that Black history didn't start in slavery, and it sure wouldn't end in poverty.

I told them the truth, that their very existence was resistance. I carried with me not just scripture but legacy. I poured out what had been poured into me, drawing from deep wells of memory, of lynchings whispered about behind closed doors, of Black businesses that once stood on streets long since paved over, of mothers who held it together with nothing but prayer and dishwater hands.

And every time I took that microphone, whether in a pulpit or a school auditorium, I wasn't just giving a speech. I was demanding a charge. I was declaring that our history is not a burden, it's a blueprint.

In 2004, life reminded me just how fragile even the strongest vessel can be. I was behind the wheel one afternoon, cruising down the familiar backroads of Ringgold, roads I had traveled for decades, gravel kicking up beneath my tires, pine trees waving like old friends. The sun was out, and the day was ordinary until it wasn't. Without warning, everything went black.

Just for a moment, but long enough. The world vanished, no sound, no light, just a blank slate where consciousness had been. I came back to myself, confused and shaken, my hands still on the steering wheel, heart racing, sweat beading down my neck. I pulled over and sat there, breathing heavily, trying to make sense of what had just happened.

I told myself it was probably nothing. Just fatigue. Maybe low blood sugar. I was in my seventies now, these things happen. But then it happened again. And again.

The episodes became more frequent. Sudden blackouts, like a light switch flipped off and back on. I could feel myself disappearing, and I didn't know if I would come back each time. That's when I knew, I couldn't ignore this. Something was wrong.

I went to the VA hospital. I sat in a waiting room surrounded by old warriors like myself, men who had once worn uniforms and carried rifles, now carrying oxygen tanks, canes, and silent burdens. I filled out the paperwork and told them what was happening. They didn't waste time. I was referred immediately to LSU Medical Center in Shreveport for a full work-up.

What followed was a gauntlet, scans, blood work, specialists, poking and prodding, questions I couldn't answer. I lay inside machines that hummed and clicked, metal tubes that scanned the very blueprint of my brain. I had taught science once, long ago, but now I was the experiment.

And then the news came. The doctor sat me down, white coat, serious eyes, clipboard in hand, and told me that they had found a tumor. Not just any tumor. It was hidden deep behind my nasal cavity, pressed up close against the nerves that controlled my vision, my balance, and my very consciousness. A brain tumor.

I didn't flinch. I didn't panic. I had been through too much already to be shaken by one more trial. God had brought me through segregation, the war, integration battles, the deaths of my parents, prostate cancer, and more heartbreaks than I could count. I didn't get scared, I got still. I nodded. "Okay," I told him. "What next?" They told me surgery was required. But not the kind where they cut open your skull and lay your mind bare, no, this would be a nasal entry procedure, a delicate operation that involved threading instruments through my nose and extracting the tumor by suction. Precision work. A risk, yes, but a miracle of modern medicine.

And so, I lay back. I let the doctors do what they were trained to do. But even as they prepared the tools and sterilized the room, I knew in my heart that the real healing was already underway. Because I wasn't just going under the knife, I was going under the hand of God.

They put me under anesthesia, and when I woke up, it was done. The tumor was gone, removed in full. The surgeons told me the operation was a success, textbook, they said. No complications. No damage to surrounding nerves. No infections. Nothing.

I never had another blackout again. Not one. I thanked the doctors for their skill. I shook their hands. But in my heart, I knew who the real Physician was. It was God who guided their hands. God, who had revealed the tumor before it took me. God, who had kept me on the road that day instead of letting me drift into a ditch or worse. God, who let me walk out of that hospital with a clear mind and a whole heart.

Because that's how God works sometimes, not always in thunder and lightning, but in surgical suites and quiet recoveries. That experience changed me. Not in the way trauma does, but in the way grace does. It reminded me that every breath is borrowed. Every moment is a gift. And that even when the body fails, the Spirit stands ready. I walked out of LSU Medical Center with a scar you couldn't see but a story you could feel. And to this day, I carry it not as a wound, but as a witness.

From 2005 to 2007, I stayed active in ministry. I wasn't preaching from a big pulpit, but I was preaching just the same, visiting homes, praying with families, counseling young men, and showing up wherever the Lord told me to go. I had hung up my barber clippers by then, but I still found joy in gardening, giving food from our land to neighbors and elders, and mentoring boys who didn't know their worth yet.

Then came 2008. The year the world tilted just a little bit closer to justice. The year hope, real, living, breathing hope, stepped into the spotlight. And this time, hope looked like *us*.

That November, I watched history unfold, not on the battlefields of war, not in the streets of protest, but through the soft hum of my television, right in the center of my living room. I sat in my favorite chair, back straight, hands folded, remote untouched, as the final election results rolled in. Red and blue maps turned gray and then certainty. States began falling like dominoes, one by one until it happened: Barack Hussein Obama was declared the forty-fourth president of the United States. I didn't leap. I didn't shout. I cried. Not the kind of crying that sneaks out quietly. No, these were heavy, body-rocking tears. The kind of tears that come from your soul, not your eyes.

I saw in that moment more than just a man on a stage. I saw a mirror reflecting all the people who had carried us to this point. I saw my grandfather, Alfred Daniels, born in 1872, just nine years after Lincoln signed the Emancipation Proclamation. A man who never knew true freedom, even though the law said he was free.

I saw my mother, Lucille, bent over White folks' laundry, scrubbing their stains out so she could feed five children on nickels and faith. I remembered her hands, cracked from bleach and water, raised every Sunday in worship anyway.

I saw my students, the little Black boys they said wouldn't amount to anything, the Black girls whose braids were too tight and dreams too big. I saw them in the crowd that night, their faces lit by cellphone screens and tears, chanting *"Yes we can"* not as a slogan but as a song of deliverance.

I thought about the marches, the jail cells, the night rides, the bombed churches, and the funerals with no headlines. I thought of the Tuskegee Airmen who flew higher than segregation told them they could. I thought of the Little Rock

Nine, walking through crowds that spit like vipers to get to algebra class.

I thought of Dr. King, who dreamed of this moment in technicolor while facing it in black and white. He never made it to this day, but I did. We did.

I thought of the signs that once hung in diners and bus stops: "Whites Only." "No Coloreds Allowed." And now here we were, watching a Black man step into the highest house in the land. Not as a janitor. Not as a servant. Not as a guest. But as commander-in-chief.

I saw Michelle standing next to him, Black, beautiful, brilliant. I saw those little girls in their bright dresses, skipping across a stage built by the bones of people who couldn't even vote. I thought about what their presence meant, what it would mean to little Black girls who had never seen themselves reflected in power, only punished by it. And I whispered, with a full heart and a trembling voice:

"Thank You, Lord." Because this wasn't just history. This was prophecy fulfilled.

This was "*We the People*" rewritten in our image. This was the dream, knocking on the door of reality and being told, "Come in. We've been waiting for you."

It didn't erase the struggle. It didn't fix everything.

But it *meant* something. It meant we weren't crazy for holding on. It meant our prayers hadn't fallen on deaf ears. It meant that our labor, our mourning, our marching, our mentoring, was not in vain.

That night, I sat a little taller in my chair. Not because we had "arrived" but because we had survived long enough to *witness*. And witnessing my friend, that's holy. But just eight years later, in 2016, the nation swung hard in the opposite direction.

After the soaring hope of President Obama, we watched in disbelief as Donald J. Trump, the man who had built his brand on division, celebrity, and controversy, stepped into the White House. He defeated Hillary Clinton, a woman many believed was next in line, someone with decades of experience and the potential to build on Obama's legacy. Instead, America chose a man who stoked fears, amplified hate, and seemed determined to unravel progress like a thread from a hem.

I remember watching the results roll in that November night, this time not with joy, but with a deep, unsettled ache. The same television that had lit my living room with hope in 2008 now flickered with headlines that made my stomach turn. I wasn't surprised, not entirely. But I was disappointed. Deeply. It felt like we had taken two steps forward and been shoved ten steps back.

And it wasn't just about politics, it was about principle. The tone of the country changed overnight. Rhetoric got sharper. Tempers flared. Old prejudices that had once whispered now shouted from podiums and screens. I had lived through Jim Crow, through segregation, through governors standing in schoolhouse doors, and still, something about this moment felt just as dangerous. Because it wasn't coming from the margins, it was coming from the top.

I thought of my children. My grandchildren. I thought of every young person I had ever mentored, every student I had ever told, "You can be anything." And now I wondered if the country would let them.

But even in that climate, I didn't lose hope. No man, no matter how loud or powerful, could change who I served. I had seen too much of God's hand to be shaken by man's election. Power on earth may shift, but power in heaven is constant.

So I prayed. I preached. And I warned. Because I knew the storm wasn't over, it had just changed direction.

The climate in America had grown tense again. Old wounds reopened. Hard truths resurfaced. But I didn't let that pull me into despair. I'd lived through darker times and seen God's hand move in them all. If anything, the times only sharpened my sense of urgency. I had work to do, souls to reach, stories to tell, seeds to plant.

From 2010 through 2014, I stayed on assignment. I entered my eighties with strength in my limbs and fire in my bones. I wasn't always behind a pulpit, but I was always preaching. On porches and in parking lots, at revivals and funerals, in the produce aisle, at fish fries and family reunions, I carried the Word like a farmer carries his best seed: ready to sow wherever the ground was soft.

My health was strong. My mind was clear. My garden was flourishing, and my prayers still had power. I fed the hungry with what grew in my soil, and I fed the weary with what grew in my spirit. If someone needed a ride to the doctor, I gave it. If they needed to be reminded that they mattered, I told them. I was retired from the school system, but not from purpose.

And yet, in all my activity, I could feel something shifting. The world was loud with distractions, churches focused more on performance than power, and people chased platforms instead of presence. Something in my spirit began to stir. I didn't know what it was at the time, but I could feel God getting my attention in a new way.

Then came 2015. In 2015, something happened that turned my world upside down, or maybe right-side up. It was a night like any other, or so it seemed. The kind of night that slips in quiet and uneventful, wrapped in the stillness that only comes after a day of honest labor, a warm meal, and scripture before bed. I was lying beside Sarah, just as I had done for decades. That bed, our bed, had held our prayers, our dreams, our tears. It had carried me through surgeries, through restless nights after burying my parents, through whispered thank-yous to a God who kept on keeping me. But nothing in that bed could have prepared me for what was about to happen.

The air changed first. It was subtle at first, like a shift in pressure when a storm is coming. The kind of silence that doesn't feel empty but *charged*. A thickness in the air that wrapped around me like a presence, one I couldn't see but *felt* with every fiber of my being. And then it happened, sudden, sovereign, and silent. I was lifted. Not startled. Not jerked. Lifted.

I wasn't dreaming. I wasn't delirious. I was *awake*. Fully aware. My eyes open, my mind sharp. Yet somehow, my body was no longer under its own power. I was rising, slowly, reverently, like invisible hands had scooped me from beneath and whispered to my soul, *"Be still."*

I didn't fight it. I didn't flinch. I felt no fear. Only awe.

The ground beneath me disappeared, but I never fell. I wasn't walking, I was being *carried*. Gently. Like something holy had chosen me for a moment beyond comprehension. I floated, yes, floated, out of my bedroom, through the quiet hallway, and into my living room. That familiar space, with the old recliner where I read the Word, where I sipped sweet tea, where I wept for my children, where I had preached to empty rooms to get the Word out of me, it all felt different. It didn't feel like my house. It felt like *a sanctuary*. And then the presence stopped moving me. I was seated in my chair, *placed* there, not dropped, and then it came. A voice. Not loud, but *impossible to ignore*. Not harsh, but filled with power. It didn't echo off the walls, it *settled* into the very core of the room. A voice with no face, no accent, no hesitation. Just *truth*.

And that voice, clearer than thunder, smoother than water, spoke three short sentences. That was all. But those three sentences still echo in me to this day. "Guard your heart." "Jesus is coming back soon." "The churches today are not living right, and they need to get right."

I didn't see wings. I didn't see fire. But I knew what I had just experienced. It was an angel, not the kind you paint on church fans or print on sympathy cards. No robe, no halo. Just authority. Just presence. A messenger of the Most High sent not to entertain me but to *enlist* me. Because those words weren't suggestions, they were *orders*.

I sat there in stunned silence. My body trembled, not out of fear, but out of reverence. I thought of Moses at the burning bush, Isaiah in the temple, and John on the Isle of Patmos. And now here I was, a Black man in Ringgold, Louisiana, sitting in my living room, receiving divine dispatch like I was one of them, not because I was worthy but because God still had work for me.

The first instruction, "Guard your heart", hit deep. I had seen enough in my lifetime to know that the heart is a battlefield. Bitterness, pride, distraction, ego, those things sneak in unnoticed. Even church folks fall prey. We guard our wallets, our phones, our reputations, but we leave our hearts wide open to corruption. That word reminded me: *if the heart goes, everything goes.*

The second, "Jesus is coming back soon", wasn't new information. I'd preached it. I'd read it in Revelation. But this time, it wasn't just theology. It was *urgent*. The signs were already around us, natural disasters, wars, racial unrest, and truth traded for popularity. I didn't need a headline to confirm it. I had just heard it straight from heaven.

And the third, "The churches today are not living right, and they need to get right", cut the deepest. Because I had seen it. I had watched the church shift over the decades. Once a place of power, refuge, and revival, it is now diluted by politics, performance, and pride. Some preachers are chasing fame instead of lost souls. Some pulpits are without substance, louder in sound but empty in substance. Choirs are full, but prayer closets are empty. We had learned how to *look* churchy but forgotten how to *be* holy.

That angel's voice was not condemning, it was corrective. It was a divine reminder that the church was still God's bride, but she needed to prepare herself for the return of the Bridegroom.

When the presence lifted, the room felt empty, but my spirit felt *full*. I sat in that chair for what seemed like hours. I couldn't move. I didn't want to. I just sat there and changed. The television was off. The lights were dim. But I had never seen more clearly. That encounter wasn't meant to elevate me. It was meant to *ignite me.*

At that point, I had lived through almost nine decades, through war, segregation, cancer, loss, injustice. I had stood in front of classrooms and congregations. I had laid hands on the sick and cried at my parents' graves. I thought I had seen it all. But that visitation reminded me *God's not done with you just because you've lived a long life. He's just getting started.*

From that moment forward, I walked differently. I preached differently. I prayed like every word mattered. I taught like time was short. Because it is. That angel didn't come to pat me on the back. He came to put fire in my bones. And I've been burning ever since.

From 2015 through 2017, I lived with a fire that wouldn't go out. That angelic visitation hadn't just stirred me, it had recommissioned me. I was no longer living out of routine, I was living on assignment. Every breath I took felt like a borrowed blessing. Every step I made, every word I spoke, felt charged with divine purpose. I wasn't just an old man in a small town, I was a vessel of warning, wisdom, and *witness*.

I didn't need a pulpit to preach. Wherever I was, the Word followed. Sometimes, it was on the porch with a group of young men, slouched in folding chairs, heads bowed not in prayer but in quiet curiosity. I'd speak the truth anyway. Sometimes, it was in the produce aisle of the local store, right there next to the collard greens, reminding someone that Grace still had their name on it. Sometimes, it was in a hospital room, sitting beside someone whose body was failing but whose spirit could still be stirred.

And my garden, oh, the garden was still thriving. Even in my eighties, I'd get up early, till the soil, and drop seed into the earth like I was praying over it. Peas, okra, corn, greens, it wasn't just food; it was *ministry*. I gave away more than I kept. I'd bag up fresh vegetables and deliver them to elders who couldn't get out, single mothers stretched thin, or neighbors I barely knew. Not because I wanted a thank-you but because that's what a servant does, he gives what he's been given.

I watched the world around me shift. Churches grew flashier, but sometimes emptier. People knew more scripture but seemed to live less of it. Social media made everyone a preacher, but few lived what they posted. The news was filled with stories of violence, corruption, division, and the love of many had grown cold. But I stayed steady.

I didn't panic. I positioned myself.

I knew that when the world got darker, the light of God's people had to shine brighter. So I stayed lit. I stayed available. I told every young man and woman who sat at my feet the same thing: "Your gift ain't just for you. It's for somebody else's deliverance."

God didn't bring you through depression, addiction, brokenness, or loss just so you could post about it. He brought you through so you could pull someone else out.

The years were sacred. Steady. Rooted. Not flashy, but *faithful.* There weren't always crowds. The invitations slowed. The spotlights dimmed. But I had learned long ago: when the audience leaves, *the assignment remains.*

God had shown me too much, spared me too many times, and entrusted me with too many testimonies to stop now. So, I pressed forward. Quietly. Boldly. Consistently. Because obedience doesn't retire, purpose doesn't expire. And if your heart is still beating, God ain't done.

But just when I thought I had outlived every danger, endured every hardship, and learned every lesson life had to teach, the summer of 2018 came crawling at me with wings and a sting. I wasn't prepared, not for the pain, not for the fall, and certainly not for the humbling that followed. Funny how the smallest things can bring the biggest trials. It wasn't a car crash. It wasn't cancer. It wasn't a brain tumor. It was a wasp. It was a hot, quiet day, the kind where the sun sits heavy on your shoulders, and the heat rises off the pavement like breath. I had just come outside to move around, to get my joints working, and my spirit lifted. Even in my nineties, I liked to keep active. I wasn't out there doing layups, but I was bouncing a basketball, loosening my knees, feeling the rhythm of life echo through that familiar leather against the concrete. It was my way of reminding the world, and myself, that I was still in the game. Still here. Still moving.

Then, out of nowhere, it came. A wasp. Big, red, and angry looking. It circled me like it was sizing me up. I waved it off once, then twice. I thought it would move on. But it didn't. That thing came at me with purpose. It stung me hard on the arm. The pain was so sharp it felt like lightning kissed my skin. Instinct kicked in. I swatted that thing down and raised my leg, too quick, too high, too proud, planning to finish it off with my foot. But in that one motion, my body betrayed me. My balance shifted. My heel lost grip. And before I could catch myself, I was falling.

It wasn't like the slow-motion falls you see in the movies. It was sudden, jarring, and final. My back hit the ground first. Then came the shockwave of pain shooting through my side like a train jumping the track. Something inside me broke, clean and deep. I couldn't move. I couldn't speak. The sky above me blurred into a swirl of blue and fear. I broke my hip.

The pain was instant. And unrelenting. It wasn't just pain, it was fire. My whole body clenched, muscles locked in protest. My mouth opened to call out, but I didn't have the strength. All I could do was lie there, breathing shallow, trying not to panic, trying not to cry. Not from the pain, but from the helplessness. A ninety-year-old man, laid out by a wasp.

But God is never late, and He never leaves you alone.

Not long after, Beckie Murray, my daughter-in-law, Kendell's wife, came around the side of the house and saw me. Her face shifted from curiosity to concern in a blink. She rushed over to me, knelt down with urgency in her hands, and called Kendell. When my son arrived, they moved like clockwork. There was no hesitation or confusion, just love in action. They lifted me as carefully as they could, tears in their eyes and grit in their jaws, and got me into the car. No ambulance. No second opinions. Straight to Willis-Knighton Hospital.

The doctors didn't waste time either. They confirmed what I already knew: my hip was broken and needed replacing. Surgery was scheduled immediately. I remember the moment before they wheeled me in. I was lying flat on that hospital bed, bright lights above me, cold air on my skin. I prayed silently: "Lord, don't let this be the end. Let this be a beginning."

The surgery went well, but what followed was its own kind of trial. Recovery is no joke, especially when you've got almost a century on your bones. Rehab was grueling. Every stretch felt like punishment. Every step felt like an argument between my body and my will. They brought me a walker. Then a cane. Then, exercises that felt like a marathon. And every day, I asked God for strength, not for miracles, just for movement.

There were mornings when I wanted to quit. When I sat on the edge of the bed, I had tears in my eyes because I couldn't get my socks on. When I wondered if I'd ever walk without pain again, something in me kept pressing. That same grit that pushed me through segregation that helped me hold a family together, that carried me through surgeries and sickness, it rose up again.

Day by day, I improved. Inch by inch, I got stronger. And by April of 2019, I was back on my feet. Not running. Not dancing. But walking, with purpose. With power. With a cane in one hand and testimony in the other. I wasn't just walking, I was marching.

That cane wasn't a symbol of weakness. It was a badge of honor. It was proof that I had gone to the edge, looked over, and stepped back with my head high. I wore that cane like a crown. Each tap against the floor said: "I'm still here." Each stride whispered: "God's not done with me yet."

People ask me if I'm afraid of getting older. I tell them this: age doesn't scare me. Stillness does. And even after a fall, after pain, after months of healing, I refused to sit still. That wasp didn't win. That fall didn't finish me. That cane doesn't carry me, I carry it. Because some stories don't end with defeat. Some stories rise with the sound of footsteps and the strength of one more step. And mine? Still marching.

NOT FINISHED YET (2020–2024)

By the time 2020 rolled around, Sarah and I had already made one of the most complicated spiritual decisions of our lives. After nearly eight decades of faithful service, first as members of Liberty Hill CME Church and later as leaders of Liberty Hill Outreach, we closed the church doors that had been my soul's anchor since 1941. That decision didn't come with headlines or parades. It came with tears, whispered prayers, and the sacred weight of knowing when to let something rest. We hadn't failed; we had fulfilled our assignment. And just like a good servant who lays down his tools at the end of the day, we stepped away, with gratitude in our hearts and peace in our spirits.

Liberty Hill wasn't just a church. It was a living chronicle of Black endurance and praise. Those wooden pews held our elders during Jim Crow, our children during school integration, and our family during every chapter in between. I preached there. Prayed there. Buried loved ones there. My children had grown up under its tin roof, cut their teeth on its hymns, and learned how to pray at its wooden altar. Liberty Hill was where I learned not just about God, but where I met Him.

But the foundation had shifted, not in concrete, but in community. The saints were growing older. The younger generation had scattered like seeds to the wind, some for opportunity, some from disillusionment. I tried for years to hold the line. I watered the soil. I preached with fire. I visited every shut-in, taught every child, and cleaned the grounds with my own hands. But sometimes, no matter how faithful the farmer, the field has run its course.

So we released it, not in defeat, but in faith. We entrusted Liberty Hill to memory and to heaven, believing that what was built there would echo beyond its walls.

We transitioned to Hebrew Baptist Church, the same church where Sarah had grown up as a young girl, her dress neatly pressed, Bible tucked under her arm, and a quiet sense of purpose still waiting to unfold. For her, it was a homecoming; for me, it was a kind of resurrection. The first time I stepped through those doors, I felt something I hadn't felt in a long time, not just familiarity but favor. There was no pomp, no production, just presence. The worship was heartfelt, the people warm and welcoming, and the Word came forth pure and uncut. It wasn't a perfect church, but it was a present one. And sometimes, that's all you need, somewhere that still knows how to tarry, how to listen, how to love.

Under the leadership of Pastor Henry Johnson, Hebrew became our new spiritual home. I didn't arrive as a stranger, nor was I treated like a retired man on the sidelines. Pastor Johnson welcomed me with open arms and gave me room to operate as the Lord leads. Though he shepherds the church with grace and vision, I remain the senior pastor in title, and I am free to preach whenever the Spirit gives me utterance. I don't take the pulpit every Sunday, but when I do, I stand not as a guest, but as one still called, still useful, still anointed for the work.

Sarah, too, stepped right back into service as if she had never left. She joined the choir again, lifting her voice not only in song but in testimony, singing with a strength that only comes from decades of trial and triumph. She now serves as one of the church's mothers, offering guidance, encouragement, and quiet wisdom to the younger women who sit where she once sat. Watching her serve, sing, and smile in that sanctuary reminds me that we are both still bearing fruit in our season. We may be older now, but we are not finished. In Hebrew, we didn't just find a new church, we found renewed purpose.

As Sarah and I began settling into a new rhythm of rest and renewed purpose, the world began unraveling. The pandemic arrived like a thief in the night, quiet at first, then suddenly everywhere. Coronavirus, a word that had never crossed my lips, became the air we breathed and the fear we carried. It swept across the globe like judgment in the book of Exodus, touching every city, every home, every life. The streets fell silent. Businesses shuttered their doors. Weddings were postponed. Funerals, once filled with choirs and casseroles, became somber online gatherings with no hugs from the deacon's wife and no gospel wails rising from the back pew. Cities stood still, wrapped in an eerie hush, like the whole world was holding its breath, waiting to see who would still be standing when the dust cleared.

But I had seen chaos before.

I remembered the ration lines of World War II, where a young Black boy learned to wait his turn behind others who had more but gave less. I had walked through segregated streets where your life could be reduced to a rumor, or erased altogether without a headline. I had seen the cities burn in '68, had watched neighborhoods crumble under the weight of crack cocaine, had seen the water rise over New Orleans after Katrina, and lived through an economy that swallowed men whole and left their families scraping to survive. I had marched. I had fasted. I had buried friends and classmates before their time. I had watched America break its promises over and over again. So no, I didn't panic. I prayed. Because faith doesn't just belong in Sunday morning praise breaks or shouted hallelujahs. Faith is what shows up when the doctor shakes his head, and the news brings no comfort. Faith is what steadies you when the government stutters and the shelves go bare. It's what you cling to when the world is unraveling, and you're trying not to unravel with it. And in those moments, I leaned on the same God who had carried me through every storm before. I didn't have fancy cameras or social media teams. But I had a Bible, a burden, and a call that still burned in my bones, and that was enough.

With church buildings closed and pulpit lights dimmed, the ministry had to move forward, and I moved it. We started hosting virtual Bible studies and prayer calls. Sometimes, five people showed up. Sometimes twenty. Folks would set their phones on the kitchen table, put them on speaker, and join in while stirring pots of beans or rocking babies to sleep. We prayed. We sang. Sometimes, folks would shout right there in their living rooms. I preached from my recliner. Led devotion from the same table where I'd eaten cornbread and greens for decades. My house became a sanctuary. The Word still went forth. Because the Gospel doesn't require stained glass or marble floors, it just needs someone willing to carry it.

And people were hungry. Not for potlucks or punch bowls, but for comfort, clarity, and truth. They were scared and grieving, isolated and overwhelmed. But I knew the medicine they needed could still be delivered, even through a phone line or a whispered prayer.

As restrictions began to ease and the world crept cautiously toward reopening, God wasn't finished stretching me. One morning during my prayer time, I heard His voice as clear as sunrise: "If they won't come to the church, take the church to them." So I did.

When it finally became safe to gather again, after the worst of the pandemic had passed and the world dared to breathe a little easier, I began going door to door and church to church, just like the early believers in the book of Acts. I didn't carry tracts. I carried presence. I stood on porches and offered prayer. I delivered bags of vegetables pulled from my garden that very morning. I sat in silence when no words were needed, and I lifted my voice when they were. I preached in backyards and front rooms. Some people cried. Some just nodded. But every one of them knew: they had not been forgotten. Because when the world forgets who she is, the church must remember.Even so, life has a way of humbling us when we least expect it.

Just as the world was beginning to find its footing again after the pandemic, I received yet another reminder that storms don't always come with thunder. Sometimes, they come on clear days, after birthday cake and quiet prayers.

At this stage, after nearly a century of living, you begin to believe you've seen it all. You think you've weathered every storm, survived every trial, and outlived every kind of danger that could befall a man. You start to believe your heart has already heard every sound it could make, grief, joy, heartbreak, laughter, sorrow, hope. But on that day, what happened shook me in a way I hadn't felt in many years. It reminded me that no matter your age, there are still moments that can take your breath away, not just in fear, but in awe.

In 2022, just two days after I celebrated my ninety-third birthday, God reminded me, once again, that His hand was still resting firmly on my life. Sarah and I had spent that afternoon in Lakeside, visiting an old classmate of mine. We laughed like we were back in high school, sitting in the sun and swapping stories older than most of the people left to hear them. We reminisced about Liberty Hill, about the red clay roads of our childhood, about the ones who had gone on and the few who were still holding on. There was joy in that visit, a sacred joy. The kind that only comes when you've lived long enough to truly appreciate what it means to simply still be here.

The ride home was ordinary, quiet, and clear. Sarah was driving, and we were passing down Milam Street through the 2700 block, a stretch of road we'd traveled more times than I could count. The sun was beginning to set, throwing a warm golden light across the pavement. The houses we passed looked peaceful in their stillness. We were talking gently, coasting through memory. Then, without warning, everything changed. We were hit head-on.

It wasn't a swerve or a bump, it was a violent, jarring collision. One minute, we were drifting through conversation, and the next, we were thrust into chaos. Metal shrieked and twisted like aluminum foil. Glass shattered. Airbags exploded. The car crumpled like it had been punched by an invisible hand. The noise was indescribable, an eruption of destruction, of force, of confusion. I remember the sharp smell of burning rubber, the bitter dust from the airbags, and the faint scent of blood in the air. My body jolted, then froze. Time seemed to slow down into fragments. I looked over and saw Sarah gripping the wheel, her face stunned but conscious. Then came the stillness, that eerie, ringing silence that follows trauma.

Our 2014 Toyota was totaled. The front end was obliterated and the hood curled upward like a clenched fist. And yet, somehow, we were still sitting there, alive. No broken bones. No loss of consciousness. No final words spoken. Just breath. Still in our bodies.

The Emergency Medical Technicians rushed to the scene expecting to find the worst. But instead of tragedy, they found two older people, stunned and trembling but upright and talking. One of them wrapped a bandage around my left arm where I had a minor scrape, that was the only injury I walked away with. Sarah, though shaken to her core, had no lasting harm. No internal injuries. No broken bones. Nothing showed up on the X-rays. The doctors examined us carefully as if they couldn't believe what they were seeing. They kept looking at us like we were an unanswered question.

We were discharged that same day. No overnight stay. No surgery. No need to call the family in. We walked out of that hospital with the clothes we came in wearing and a story that would live far longer than any scar. As I stepped out of that ER, I turned to Sarah and said something I've said in many pulpits before, but never with more conviction: "God's not done with me yet."

Because I've buried people for less, I've stood behind caskets and tried to find words for families grieving children, siblings, or spouses lost to accidents far less violent than the one we had just survived. I've watched wreckage claim lives and leave nothing behind but wrecked families and unanswered prayers. I've seen people die on roads they drove every day, in neighborhoods they knew by heart. But at ninety-three years old, I walked away with a scratch and a story. And you don't walk away from something like that to go back to television and sweet tea. You walk away to testify. I knew without a doubt that God had extended my time, not by chance, but by choice. That wreck wasn't just an event. It was a message. It was confirmation that I still had purpose, that my work was not yet complete. My hands may be wrinkled now, but they still have the strength to serve. My voice may be weathered, but it still carries a word. My legs may move slower, but they still know the path. I could not sit back. I would not rest. So I stood up. Because when death comes knocking, and God answers the door with a firm, "Not yet," you don't waste that gift. You use it. You share it. You praise louder. You preach harder. You press on.

In 2023, just one year after surviving a head-on collision, the Lord gave me another assignment at the age of ninety-four, one I hadn't asked for but one I couldn't ignore. I was called to pastor St. Mary Baptist Church in Ringgold, Louisiana. It wasn't a glamorous invitation, and it didn't come with banners or a search committee. It came as a quiet whisper from heaven, unmistakable in its urgency. I answered the call the way I always have, with reverence, humility, and a willingness to serve.

St. Mary wasn't what it used to be. There was a time when that church rang with life: when the choir robes swayed to the rhythm of the Hammond organ, when the deacons' prayers thundered like storms from the pulpit, and when the aisles filled with saints, some rocking babies on their hips, others waving handkerchiefs like battle flags of praise. But by the time I arrived, the sanctuary had fallen quiet. The pews were dusted not just with age but with spiritual neglect. The congregation was small and faithful but fractured. It didn't take long to sense that the glory that once lived there had grown faint. This was a house of worship in need of revival.

I didn't come in with titles or plans to build a following. I didn't show up to entertain or grow a brand. I came to work. I came to teach. I came to serve. My mission wasn't to impress, it was to reintroduce the Word of God to a people who had grown used to routine and ritual but had drifted too far from relationship. They were used to short sermons, clean, polite, and surface-deep. What I gave them was Scripture, raw and unfiltered. I gave them the truth, whether they were ready or not. Some squirmed under the weight of it. Some resisted. But others? They came alive. I saw tired eyes widen with revelation. I saw that the Bibles were opened not just to be read but also to be studied and applied. I didn't sugarcoat it. I didn't soften the edges. I preached with discipline, clarity, and conviction, the Word that cuts deep but heals deeper. Because the church was never meant to be a stage, it was meant to be a training ground. We don't need performance. We need power. And even at ninety-four years old, I still had fire in my bones. My steps may have slowed, but my mission had not. I knew I was standing on divine assignment every time I stood behind that pulpit. The Lord was still using me, and I intended to be usable.

Then, during that season, without asking, campaigning, or expecting, I received recognition that touched me in a way few things ever have. I was awarded an Honorary Doctorate of Theology. Now, I didn't need a degree to validate my calling. I've long known that my anointing wasn't earned in lecture halls, it was forged in hospital rooms, revival tents, funeral homes, and on front porches with brokenhearted souls. My theology was shaped in the trenches of life, in both heartbreak and hallelujah. But receiving that doctorate still stirred something profound inside, not pride, but peace. It reminded me that heaven sees what others overlook.

God sees the sermons preached to nearly empty rooms. He sees the scriptures studied by lamplight after long days. He sees the prayers whispered over crying children, the funerals led for families who couldn't afford the service, and the hours spent encouraging the hopeless when no one else was watching. He sees the obedience, the tears, the quiet sacrifices that never make headlines. And when heaven claps for you, it doesn't matter who else is in the room. That honorary degree wasn't for show. It was a seal. A reminder that my labor had not been in vain. That even in my nineties, I was still God's man.

In 2024, my family gave me a gift I will never forget. But before that sacred surprise, they gave me something else, a journey steeped in fellowship, memory, and love. My next-door neighbor, Joette Daniels Miles, and her sister Cassandra Daniels, the granddaughters of my Uncle Luke, joined my daughter Jackie White and her husband Jerry to take me on a road trip to Atlanta, Georgia. Our destination: the home of Nickisha Taylor and Washington Franklin, friends of my son Roy Jr., who had become more than friends, they had become family. That house didn't just welcome us, it embraced us. The laughter poured like sweet tea, and the conversations ran deep, about life, legacy, and the winding road that had brought us all to that shared moment. There was food, joy, and belonging that didn't need explanation. It was balm for the soul. But that wasn't the end of it.

A day or so later, Joette and Nickisha came to me with big grins and a vague plan. They said we needed to make a quick stop at a "work site" Nickisha was checking on. Just a little detour, they said. Nothing major. But I know my people, and I know when I'm being handled. Still, I got in the car, grumbling the whole way.

"Now, what kind of construction y'all dragging me to? This ain't the time of day for nobody to be out in the sun poking around some foundation." I fussed. I waved my hand, shook my head, and mumbled the way only an older man with a long history and a short fuse can do when he suspects he's not getting the whole story. I was suspicious, hot, and half-ready to demand we turn around.

But they just smiled, eyes forward, giving me nothing.

Then, the road curved. The trees parted. And something in the air shifted. I looked up and saw the gates, the sign. Tuskegee University. My breath caught in my throat. The grumbling stopped mid-sentence. My words fell away like dust in the wind. I couldn't speak. I couldn't move. All I could do was stare.

The tires rolled across that sacred campus, and everything in me stilled. I had only seen Tuskegee in books, in documentaries, in photographs worn smoothly with time. It was a place I had dreamed of, a temple of Black brilliance, of history and defiance and excellence. I had carried that dream like a sealed envelope in my chest, never daring to open it. And now, I was here.

I stepped out of the car slowly, not because of my age, but because I knew I was on holy ground. I could feel the weight of it, not as a burden but as a blessing. The wind even felt different, like it carried voices. I heard whispers of ancestors, of marching boots and gospel songs, of sermons and science, of freedom spoken into being by people who dared to believe they could build something eternal.

Joette and Nickisha didn't say a word. They didn't have to. The land was talking now. The bricks. The walkways. The legacy. And I, an old man who had seen segregation up close and personal, who had been denied and diminished and disregarded, was now walking across the campus of Tuskegee University with a cane in my hand and tears in my eyes.

This wasn't just a visit. It was prophecy fulfilled. It was a place I had dreamed of, prayed about, spoken of with reverence, but never stepped foot on. Tuskegee University. The moment the tires rolled across that sacred soil, I felt its weight, not as a burden, but as a mantle. The weight of history. Of honor. Of sacrifice. While standing and looking, I knew I was standing on holy ground.

This was the same ground where Booker T. Washington built an institution with bare hands and fierce vision. This was the training ground of the Tuskegee Airmen, Black men who had been told they would never fly and who soared anyway, writing their defiance in the skies. This was the place built from the ashes of slavery, fortified through segregation, and uplifted by generations of Black excellence. And now, I was standing in that legacy.

As my cane tapped against the stone pathway, I realized I wasn't walking alone. Every ancestor inside me was walking, too. Phyllis Cruel, my great-grandmother, born into bondage. Papa Alfred Daniels, my grandfather, who tilled the land with calloused hands and built a legacy from red clay and faith. My mother, Lucille, who scrubbed White folks' floors so I could have a better life. Every student I had ever taught. Every sermon I had ever preached. Every child I had ever blessed and prayed over. We were all there, walking that path together.

I didn't say a word. I didn't need to. I let the silence speak. I let the ground beneath my feet preach a sermon of its own. I could almost hear the voices of students long gone, their lessons echoing through open windows. I could hear the rhythm of marching boots, the harmony of chapel choirs, and the whispers of hope rising between those brick buildings laid by Black hands. Tears welled in my eyes, not tears of sorrow, but of awe.

At that moment, I felt the full weight of how far I had come. I remembered the cotton fields of Louisiana. I remembered drinking from "colored" fountains and riding in the back of buses. I remembered being handed schoolbooks discarded by White schools. I remembered being called "boy" even as I buried the elders of our community. And yet, there I stood, on the campus of Tuskegee, the crown jewel of Black higher education. From segregation to celebration. From closed doors to open gates. From being counted out to being counted on.

I stood still, breathed deep, and whispered not in shame but in triumph: "I am still here." Not because I was stronger. Not because I was smarter. Not because I got lucky. But because God is faithful. He kept me when bullets flew and bombs fell. He kept me through racism, through grief, through storms, through silence. He kept me when my body faltered, and my voice grew tired. And still, He called me to shine. That day at Tuskegee wasn't just a visit. It was a vindication. A sacred confirmation that every scar, every sermon, every step had led me right there. I don't take it lightly. I never will.

FINAL REFLECTIONS:

YOU CAN'T STOP ME!

If you've made it this far, then you've walked with me through the cotton fields of Louisiana, into church pews worn smooth by prayer, across battlefields and schoolrooms, through hospital corridors and revival tents, barbershops and backroads, and now into the sacred stillness of reflection.

This story ain't just about me. It's about us, every soul who ever dared to keep going when the world said "stop." It's about what it means to be born into a storm and still find the strength to build a roof. It's about making peace with your scars and learning to love the sound of your own survival.

I wasn't supposed to make it this far. Not as a Black boy born in 1929. Not through Jim Crow. Not through war. Not through broken homes and segregated schools. Not through poverty and tumors and loss. Not through highways that plowed through Black neighborhoods or systems that tried to grind the light out of me.

But I'm still here because faith will outlive fury. Because when the world tried to bury me, they didn't know I was a seed.

I've been poor but never empty. I've been alone but never abandoned. I've been broken but never beyond repair. I've been quiet but never silenced.

And if this book teaches you nothing else, let it teach you this: You can survive what they said you couldn't. You can keep your dignity when systems try to steal it. You can raise holy children in unholy times. You can serve God faithfully even when no one claps for you. You can be the answer to a prayer your great-grandmother prayed on her knees in a wooden shack a hundred years ago.

I'm not a perfect man. But I am a kept man. God kept me through every hard chapter, so I could write this one.

My hands may tremble now. My steps may be slower. But my spirit stands tall. Because I know what it cost to get here.

I know what it means to be faithful in the fields and the fire.

I know what it is to outlive injustice and still choose joy.

Since turning eighty-seven, the Lord has allowed me to celebrate each birthday with joy and gratitude. We've had banquets filled with laughter, bowling parties where the pins fell like old regrets, picnics under the Louisiana sun, and church services where the Spirit moved from pew to pulpit. Each year was another testimony, another reminder that God had not only preserved me, but kept me in purpose. He brought me from disgrace to God's amazing grace. And I don't believe He brought me this far to leave me.

If you're reading this and wondering if your life matters, it does. You don't need a stage to make an impact. You don't need applause to be anointed. Some of the strongest people I've ever known never made the news. But they made history anyway, just by not quitting.

Let them say I was stubborn. Let them say I was old-school. Let them say I never backed down. Because what they'll also have to say is: he endured. He believed. He built. He obeyed. So now I pass the baton to you. Run with it. Speak the truth. Hold your head high. Guard your heart. Love your people. Live holy. Stand firm. And whatever you do, don't stop. Because if they couldn't stop me, they sure can't stop you.

I am Roy Daniels Murray Sr. I am the son of Lucille and Bates, the grandson of Alfred and Clifford, and the great-grandson of Phyllis Cruel. I am a servant, a teacher, a fighter, a preacher, a father, a husband, and a man who refused to quit.

They tried to block me. They tried to bury me. They tried to break me.

But you can't stop me. Not because I'm strong. But because God is faithful. And His work in me is not yet finished.

BONUS CHAPTER: PHYLLIS CRUEL

You can't tell my story without starting with hers.

Phyllis Cruel was my great-grandmother, born into slavery in 1832 in Virginia, and branded with the last name of her master. That name, *Cruel*, was no accident. It was both a descriptor of the system that owned her and a testimony to what she overcame. She was never given a choice in that name. But generations later, we choose to speak it with purpose and power.

She bore five children, Minnie, George, Sarah, Martha, and Tobe, fathered by her enslaver. That kind of horror wasn't a secret back then. It was a system. The same men who claimed to be the guardians of "civilization" treated Black women like property, like vessels. But Phyllis didn't let that evil define her. She survived. She endured. And she passed on a legacy of strength, not shame.

When slavery ended in 1865, Phyllis was thirty-three years old. Still young, but already carrying the weight of multiple lifetimes. She didn't waste time looking back. She gathered her children, and at some point, made her way from Virginia to Caddo Parish, Louisiana. That journey, like so many Black migrations of the Reconstruction era, isn't recorded in detail. There are no train tickets or wagon logs to mark her path. But what we do have is this: on January 9, 1870, she stood side-by-side with a man named Jacob (Jake) Daniels, also formerly enslaved, and they were married. Legally. Freely. In the eyes of man and God.

Their marriage certificate is a sacred document in our family line. Not just because it proves a union, but because it marks the first official moment of *freedom* in our bloodline. From that union came one son: Alfred Daniels, born in 1869, just before their wedding. My *Papa*. My mother Lucille's father. The man who raised a family on eighty-three acres of land in Loggy Bayou and handed down a legacy of self-sufficiency, hard work, and faith.

Alfred Daniels would become a towering figure in our family, a landowner, a farmer, a patriarch who believed in the power of education and the value of sweat. And it all started with Phyllis. Her courage birthed generations. Her pain planted a tree whose roots are still holding strong.

I often wonder what she dreamed about, if she dared to dream. I wonder if she ever sat under a tree and imagined that her children might one day live in a world where they were free to learn, to vote, to own, to love openly without fear. Maybe she didn't get to see those dreams come true. But she dreamed them anyway.

Because I am here. Because my children are here. Because my grandchildren and great-grandchildren are here, standing on her bones, walking on the path she cleared with no map but faith.

We have searched for records, census logs, Freedmen's Bureau archives, plantation manifests, but her name doesn't appear often. Like so many Black women of her era, she was invisible to the systems that enslaved her. But she was never invisible to us. Her blood speaks. Her memory walks with me every day.

When I preach, I feel her.

When I till the earth, I honor her.

When I pray over my children and bless the next

generation, I am echoing her spirit.

Phyllis Cruel didn't live to see freedom fully realized, but

she planted it.

Her son, Alfred Daniels, built on it.

Her granddaughter, Lucille Daniels, protected it.

And I, Roy Daniels Murray, carry it forward.

We come from a line that didn't just survive, we

transformed.

We turned trauma into testimony.

We turned captivity into community.

We turned chains into churches and cotton fields into classrooms.

So when you read this book, when you walk with me through every battle, every pulpit, every schoolhouse, every family story, you are also walking with Phyllis. Because I don't walk alone.

And I don't carry my cane for balance, I carry it as a staff passed down through the generations.

The woman they tried to erase is now the reason I exist.

Phyllis Cruel Daniels. Born a slave.

Buried a matriarch.

Resurrected through every one of us.

TRIBUTES TO MR. ROY MURRAY SR.

Class Of 1977

More than a Teacher, a Mentor, a Life Coach. He prepared us academically, emotionally, and mentally for the challenges of Life. You created a supportive atmosphere of hard work, laughter, and learning.

Inspiring Educators, Business Owners, and Community Leaders alike.

Thank you, Mr. Murray, for shaping us into the Great People we are. Your sacrifices, contributions, and selflessness will continue to play a part in our lives and the lives of our children and grandchildren. "WE LOVE YOU."

Phyllis Jones Henderson, speaking on behalf of the Class of 1977

A Heartfelt Tribute to Mr. Murray
CLASS OF 1981

To Mr. Murray,

a remarkable individual who has touched our lives in countless ways. We, the Class of 1981 at Coushatta High proudly offer this heartfelt tribute. You were more than just a teacher to us; you were an educator, a mentor, a father figure, a dear friend, and a true scholar, all rolled into one.

We, the students of your Civic and World Geography classes, remember those four years at Coushatta High with immense fondness, largely thanks to you. Your classroom was a place of laughter, learning, and genuine connection. Your impact extends far beyond the classroom walls.

The gatherings, and cookouts, are not just social events. They are opportunities to relive the cherished memories we created with you. To hear your witty observations about our youthful antics, and to reaffirm the lasting impression you have made on our lives.

We the Class of 1981 "LOVE YOU."

Ethel Horton, Sylvia Wilson, Carol Giles-Davis, Anita Taylor, Lester Hall, Jerome Solton, Stephanie Babers, Roland Levi Doyle, Patricia Clark,

Randy Jackson, Lorie Moore, Greg Moore,

Billy Price, Betty Sue Allen, Peggy Demery Moore, Myra Evans, Vivan Johnson, Leon Gray, Rickey Gates, Clarence London, Brenda Harris, and so many more classmates not mentioned.

CLASS OF 1984

Mr. Murray,

Please accept our sincere gratitude for the incredible influence you had on my life and the lives of the entire class of '84. Your passion for literature was truly infectious. You possessed an unusual gift for making even the most complex texts accessible and engaging. I remember struggling until you illuminated the themes in a way that resonated deeply with me and my classmates.

You always made time for individual support, a testament to your dedication. Your unwavering belief in me, and in so many others, helped us overcome self-doubt and unlock our potential. For that, we are eternally grateful.

Dr. Donald Scott and the Class of '84.
Linda Jenkins, Debra Adams, Cathy Banks,
Henry Sibley, Felicia Babers, Annette Brown, Margaret Alford, Harold Orr, Laura Tingle,
Lee Lewis, Danny Davis, Regina Davis,
Coretta Davis, Reginald Chatman, Charlotte Cox. Etc.

CLASS OF 1985

We, the class of 1985, honor your memory. You had a great impact on our lives, influencing our learning, personal growth, and life choices. You inspired each one of us to pursue our passions. Your personality – your humor, patience, and dedication – will forever be remembered. Your legacy will live on among us.

You were more than an educator. You taught us how to step into the world that lay ahead. When we failed, you showed us how to get back up and stand firm. You listened to our problems, our goals, and our dreams, and we received invaluable counsel from you.

Your classroom was different from others. Your way of teaching was engaging for the whole room. You had a hobby that sometimes found its way into the classroom; we all know those words, and that was the defining story that tells everyone who you were.

Thank you for being a great teacher.

With Much Love & Gratitude The Class of 1985**

Janice Wilson Lewis, Ann Williams, Travis J. M. Wilson, Michael McDuffy, Zina Jones, Rita Palmer Evans, Bridget Allen Smith, Carrie Orr, Patricia Wilson Sessoms, Mary James Chandry McDuffy Lewis, and Cameo Sibley

CLASS OF 1993

To Mr. Murray, with deepest respect and gratitude,

The Class of '93 stands tall, thirty years strong, and we take this moment to collectively salute you. As we reflect on our journey since leaving the halls of (C.H.S.), your influence still remains a guiding light.

We, the Class of '93, have spread far and wide, leaving "footprints of achievement, service, and love" across various states, cities, and right here in our cherished community.

You instilled in us not just knowledge, but a spirit that resonates in our class motto, "Enough Said." It speaks about our commitment, our determination, and our unwavering pride in being Choctaws. You challenged us, encouraged us, and believed in us, even when we may have doubted ourselves.

We are forever grateful and indebted to you.

*LaShun Berry, Stephanie Brown, Anthony Davis
Latosha Smith, Marche Clark, Mandrel Jones, Calvert
Hobley, Bridgett Cole, Lecresha Richmond
Makorios Keesee, Jackie Moore, Angela Sloan
Roshawanda Taylor, Darla Bonnette, Danielle Tony, Holly
Longino, Michelle Odom, Wayne Woodard, Roger Cason,
Michael Longino, Stephanie Davis, Nicole Davis, Clyde
Wilson, Ed Taylor, Lyn Trotter, and Lafran Trotter*

LEGACY

CHRONICLES

Papa Alfred Daniels and Mama Clifford Daniels

Papa Alfred Daniels, Mama Lucille Murray,

and J.C. Daniels

Uncle Luke

Aunt Bob and Uncle Luke

Class of 1950 Ringgold Colored High School

Roy Murray Sr. in the Army

Roy Murray Sr.'s graduation from Grambling

Roy Murray Sr. at Grand Bayou

Roy Daniels Murray, Sr, and Sarah Reliford Murray

Sarah Murray

Mike and Victoria Reliford, the parents of Sarah Murray

A young Kendell

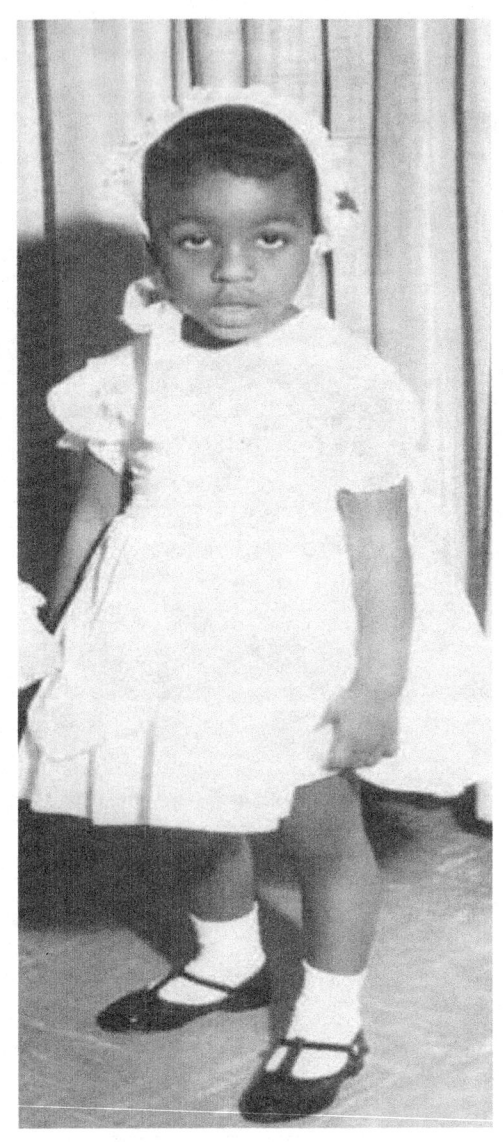

A young Jackie

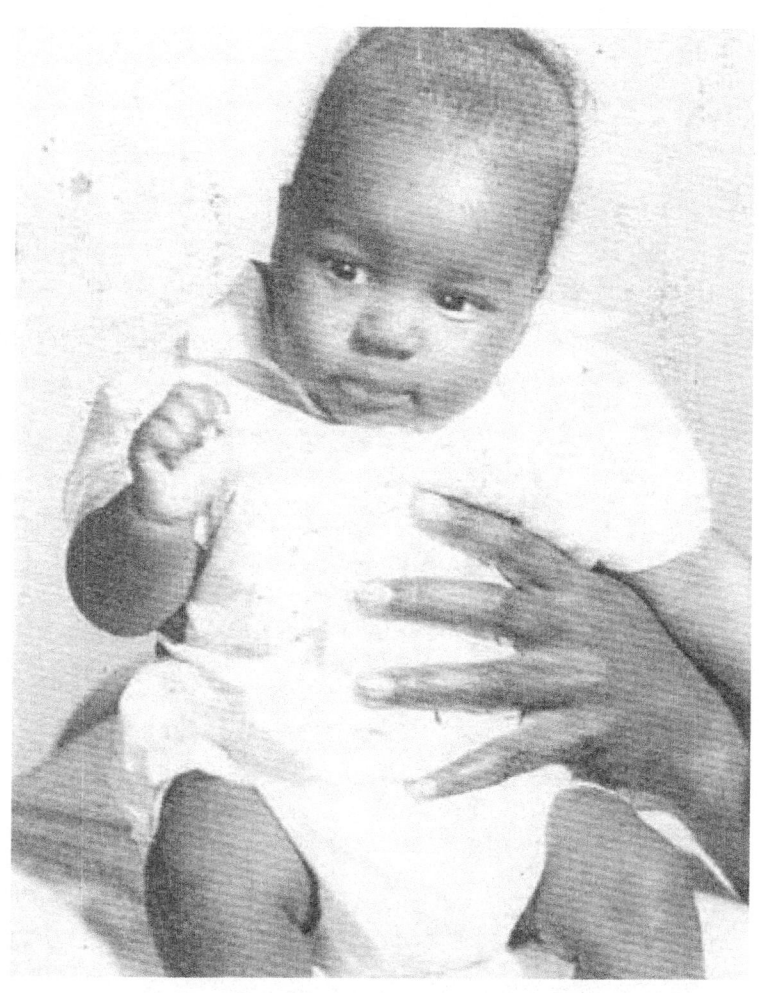

A young Roy Jr.

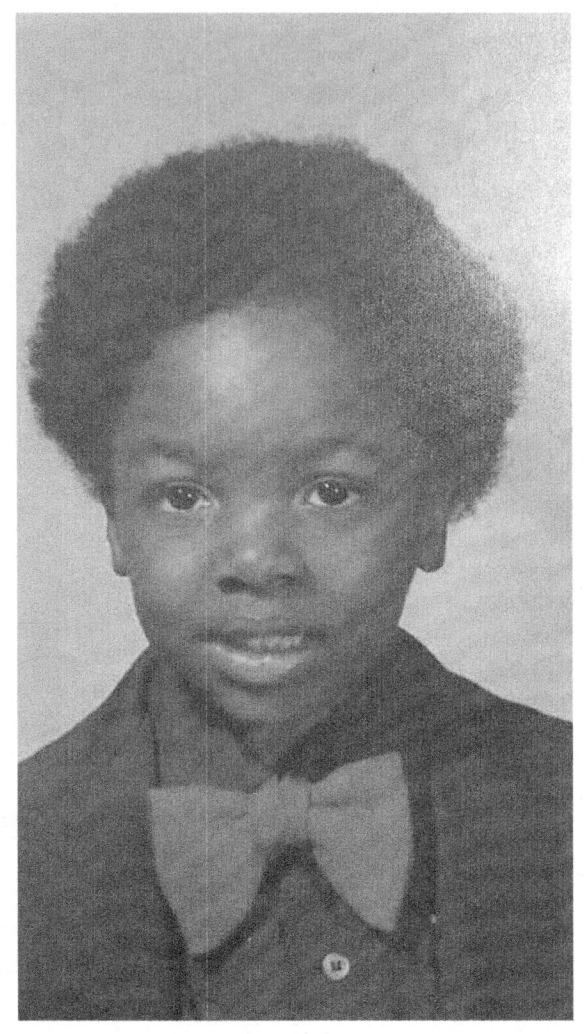

A young Patrick

Roy Sr. graduation from LSU with a Masters

Uncle Clearance and Aunt Doris

Say It Loud!!!

by Roy Murray

In any political system, there must be a communication process. There must be a medium of exchange through political socialization. There must be an understanding between the authoritative decision makers and the community.

If any segment of the community is given a deaf ear, the political machine will eventually break down. Riots and other social disruptions usually occur. We are going to be prok productive citizens. Therefore, we must properly articulate and aggregate our demands.

Until lately, we have told the central office and other decision makers what we thought they wanted to hear. We scratched our heads when they weren't itching; we laughed when there was nothing funny. From this day forward, we can lie no more. We just have to tell it like it is.

One of the best ways to communicate to our decision makers is through recruitment.

become a reality instead of a myth, the political arena must be restructured. At present, one must vote for someone he does not want in order to make his vote count for someone he wants. We have been tricked into voting for officials at large. If we demand that a certain official represent a certain precinct, our recruitment would rise.

We cannot just settle for a Black-White ratio among teachers, but we must recruit that same ratio at the central office, school board, state legislature, etc., etc., etc.

Don't just itch for Success, Scratch for it, and remember: 'Nothing is gained without work.''

LEA's Fourth Dist. To Honor Educators

Roy D. Murray, President of the Louisiana Education Association's Fourth Dist., has announced that the association will present a soiree honoring the 1970 ''Educators of the Year.''

The Annual Educators of the Year Program will be held at the Carver Branch YMCA on Saturday, May 9 from 6 p.m. to 8 p.m.

THURSDAY, APRIL 2, 1970

Teacher Power

by Roy Daniels Murray
President - Fourth District
LEA

If we want our dream ''Educational Excellence'' to become real instead of a night-mare, then it is imperative that we become actively involved. The lawyers run legal procedure, the doctors run the medics, and educators should run the education of this state and nation.

Our organization is the only one recognized by the National Education Association in the state of Louisiana. Therefore it is our responsibility to keep the torch of understanding burning during this era of change. We cannot afford idly while the 9th and 8th grade school board members shape our future.

Even though LEA is the only recognized educational association in Louisiana, we have a break down in the communication process. The primary reason for this is because of the cross-overs in the desegregation process. If we are to promote educational excellence, it is of vital importance that we relate to each other.

We must bargain from a point of strength rather than weakness. ''We must all hang together, most assuredly, we shall each hang separately.''

Teachers in Denver, Colorado demonstrated with picket signs and demanded a pay increase. Now a teacher with a masters degree can earn up to $15,000. The teachers in Los Angeles made demands and their demands were met. Chicago's starting teachers received $900 a year more than Louisiana's top master degree teachers. At the LEA Convention in Monroe in 1967, Gov. McKeithen promised us a $1500 raise over a four year period. That Monroe promise has not helped me to pay my bills.

I am not saying that a pay increase would solve all our problems, but it would give teachers a chance to devote more of their time to creative teaching. Most of our teachers have to have part-time jobs that turn up a lot of their energy badly needed in the teaching profession. Many of our new teachers are going into other occupations because of our poor salary schedule. Now, I am calling upon LEA's silent majority to become actively involved so we can meet the challenge of the 70's. I am calling upon those who say what are we going, to begin say what are we doing. It is more I and they; if it is not we.

Shreveport Sun articles written by Roy Sr., President of LEA Fourth District

Coushatta High School

Roy Murray during his teaching days in the 70s

Mama Lucille and her granddaughter Robin

Mike and Victoria Reliford, the parents of Sarah Murray

Liberty Hill Outreach Church

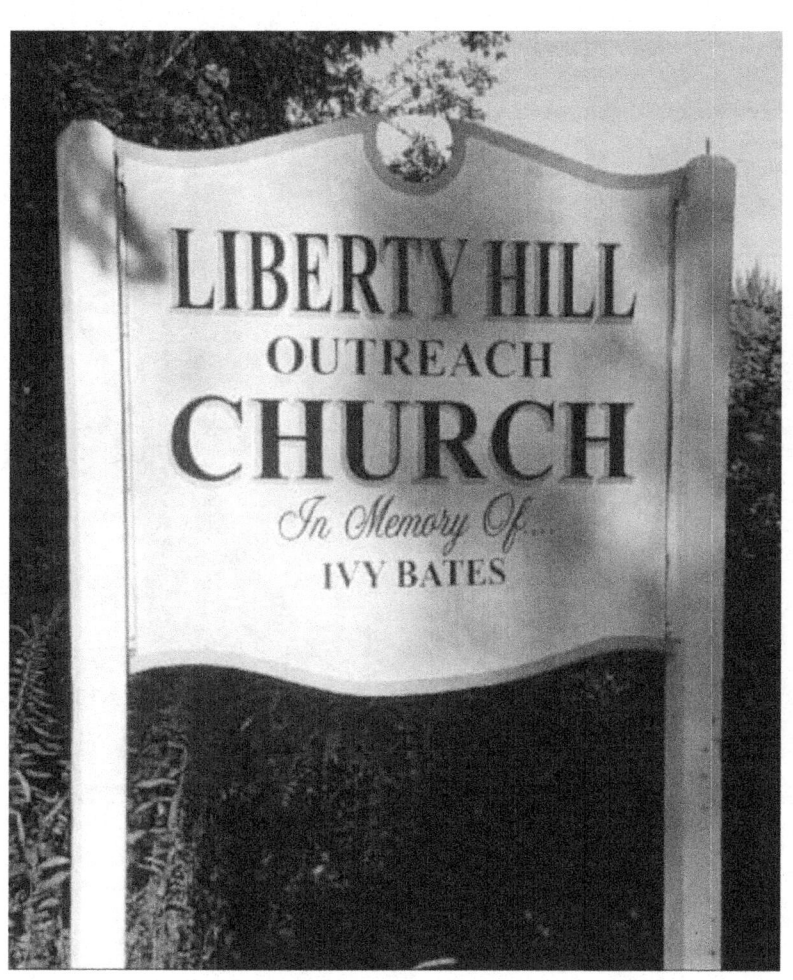

Liberty Hill Outreach Church

Aunt Helen

Roy Murray Sr Siblings: Clifford, Roy, Lee Arthur, Bates Jr.

Roy Sr at Liberty Hill Outreach

Sarah Murray

**Coushatta High Students with Roy Murray Sr
at a surprise 87th birthday party**

Roy Murray Sr, and Sarah Murray with their children on a family vacation to New Orleans: Patrick, Jackie, Kendell

Roy Sr's 95th Birthday in Loggy Bayou

Christmas in Loggy Bayou

Family & Friends Vacation in Las Vegas

Thanksgiving in Loggy Bayou: Murray & Daniels Family

346

Victoria White Moore's Wedding, the Granddaughter of Roy Sr.

Patrick, Roy Jr., Jackie, and Kendell

Kendell, Jackie, Roy Jr., and Patrick

Roy Sr. on his trip to Tuskegee

Roy Murray Sr., while thinking about Grambling

Roy Sr receives an honorary doctorate

Roy Sr on his Birthday

ABOUT THE AUTHOR: ROY MURRAY, JR.

Roy Murray Jr. is a dynamic multi-hyphenate: a seasoned IT Infrastructure and Low-Voltage Project Manager, a recording artist, a chef-entrepreneur, and now a published author.

With over 20 years of experience in project management, Roy has led high-impact technology rollouts for national brands such as BigShots Golf, Baylor University, and Texas Tech, and has managed IT and AV operations for major events, including the PPA World Championship and the **AT&T Byron Nelson**. Known for his precision, people leadership, and cross-functional communication, Roy has overseen network design, audiovisual integrations, structured cabling, and full rip-and-replace infrastructure transformations for high-profile venues and hospitality spaces across the country.

But Roy's story doesn't stop at technology. He's a **vocalist and recording artist**, having performed in jazz and blues bands and recorded several albums. His love for music is matched only by his talent in the kitchen: he founded and operated **BJ's Cajun Kitchen**, a beloved food truck known for bringing bold Southern flavors to the streets with heart and heat.

Roy is also an avid traveler who finds inspiration in exploring cultures, food, and music from around the world. He brings all these influences, technical, musical, culinary, and cultural, into everything he creates.

In 2025, Roy published his debut memoir, *Try to Block Me; You Can't Stop Me!* a powerful tribute to his father's legacy and a chronicle of Black perseverance, love, and spiritual endurance across generations. This book is not just a personal reflection; it's a historical witness.

Roy has a M.A. in English and a B.S. in Political Science, *Cum Laude*, both from **Louisiana Tech University**

From data cables to soul-stirring songs, from gumbo pots to gospel-rooted prose, Roy Murray, Jr. is a builder of systems, stories, and spirit.

CONTACT INFO

Roy Murray, Jr

6225 Sonhaven Drive, Shreveport, Louisiana 71119

📞 214-498-5815
✉ roymurrayjr@outlook.com

Made in the USA
Monee, IL
19 August 2025

22597913R00197